September

Dear PJ

Thank you for your
interest and support -
Never Again!
Joan Adler

M000249121

FOR THE SAKE
OF THE
CHILDREN

THE LETTERS BETWEEN
OTTO FRANK
AND
NATHAN STRAUS JR.

Joan Adler

Straus Historical Society, Inc.
Post Office Box 416
Smithtown, NY 11787-0416
info@straushistory.org
ISBN: 978-0-9801250-5-4

Timeline

1933

January 30: Adolph Hitler sworn in as Chancellor of the German Reich by German president Paul von Hindenburg.

February 27: The Reichstag, home of German parliament, was set on fire. Emergency powers were granted to Hitler as a result.

March: First Nazi concentration camp established at Dachau. It originally held 4,800 prisoners.

March 4: FDR sworn in as United States 32nd president.

April 1: Nazis boycott Jewish owned shops and businesses.

May 10: 20,000 books burned by German students.

July 14: Nazi Party is the only party. Nazis prohibit Jews from owning land.

1934

April 19: Heinrich Himmler becomes head of the SS.

May: Jews cannot get national health insurance or serve in the military.

June: Leadership of the Storm Troopers (S.A.) was purged of any "undesirables." This was called the "Night of the Long Knives."

1935

The United States quota for Germans immigrating to the U.S. increased to 5,532.

July 15: First pogrom - in Berlin.

Aug 31: In the U.S., The Neutrality Act of 1915 prohibited the export of arms and implements of war to belligerent countries. Provisions of the act were only for two years. It was continuously renewed thereafter. U.S. passed joint resolution of Congress.

September 1935: Nuremberg Laws passed. They stripped Jews of their citizenship and prohibited them from sexual relationships or marriage with non-Jews.

1936

The United States quota for Germans immigrating to the U.S. increased to 6,642.

March 7: Hitler's troops cross into Rhineland, a buffer zone between France and Germany. The French didn't respond militarily to this violation of the Treaty of Versailles.
August: The Olympic Games held in Berlin.

1937

United States quota for Germans immigrating to the US increased to 11,536.
January: In Germany Jews were banned from practicing their profession including teaching.
May 1: Neutrality Act expired. Cash & Carry enacted – allowing Allied nations to pay cash for American goods at American ports and then transport them away in their own ships. This act had a limit of two years.
October: FDR speech: "The peace, the freedom, and the security of ninety percent of the population is being jeopardized by the remaining ten percent who are threatening a breakdown of all international order and law."

1938

The United States accepted 7,686 German immigrants, about 10,000 fewer than the legal limit. 67% of Americans wanted refugees kept out.
March: All anti-Semitic laws in Germany extended to include the Austrians as a result of Anschluss, a political union established between Nazi Germany and Austria.
July 6: In Evian-les-Bains on the shores of Lake Geneva, representatives from 32 nations met to discuss Nazi Germany and the refugee crisis. The Evian Conference proposed by FDR reflected world opinion: country after country came forward with a reason for rejecting Jewish immigrants. Only the Dominican Republic agreed to increase their quota.
July 25: Nazis prohibit Jewish doctors in Germany from practicing medicine.
August: Nazis enact a law forcing Jewish men to add Israel to

their name and women to add Sara to theirs. Documents about Jewish people are altered to reflect this.

September 29: Germany invades Czechoslovakia without resistance.

October 1 - October 10: Germany takes control of the Sudetenland.

November 9-10: Kristallnacht takes place. Extreme violence was acted out against Jews; their places of worship and their businesses. Books, religious materials and personal items were burned.

1939

Early 1939: The waiting list for those wishing to enter the U.S. was more than 300,000. The quota for Germans to immigrate to the United States was 6,642.

May-June: The sailing of the immigrant ship St Louis shows that no country wants to take Jews.

August 20: Germany and Soviet Union sign a non-aggression pact.

September 1: Germany invades Poland signaling the beginning of World War II.

September 3: Great Britain declares war on Germany. France follows a few hours later.

November 4: Congress extends the Cash and Carry Act. This permits European countries to buy war materials.

1940

January: FDR issues a memo suggesting that, while most immigrants are honorable people, some might be spies or saboteurs

April 30: Nazis seals off the Lodz ghetto in Poland.

April-May: Germany invades Norway, Denmark, in April. Belgium, Luxembourg, Netherlands fall in May.

May 10: Winston Churchill succeeds Neville Chamberlain as Prime Minister of Britain.

June 22: France capitulates to Germany. Germany occupies France with the exception of the southeast which is called Vichy France.

June: U.S. State Department orders tighter visa controls. People need to show they have a good reason to leave their country as well as to enter the U.S. American consuls had to investigate the applicants to show they were not likely to engage in radical activities.

July 20: Battle of Britain begins.

1941

March 11: FDR signs the Lend-Lease Act. It allowed the U.S. to sell or lease materials to any country the US deems vital to its defense.

March: Further tightening of visa controls.

April 30: Otto Frank wrote to Nathan Straus Jr. asking for help getting his family out of Holland.

June: Otto Frank does not qualify for an American visa because he has close relatives still living in Germany.

June 16: U.S. requires Germany to close its consulates in the U.S.

June: Germany retaliates by requiring all American consulates to close.

June 30: Lisbon Consul General suspends action on a visa for a family that has relatives living in Belgium, Germany and the Netherlands.

July 1: Visa Division of the State Department takes over the screening process for new visa applications. New affidavit forms are required.

July 1: American Ambassador to Cuba informs the Cuban government that Americans who arrived in Cuba on tourist visas might not qualify to enter the U.S.

Aug 9-12: Churchill and FDR meet on board warships off the coast of Argentina and Newfoundland. They sign the Atlantic Charter. The agreement concerned "the final destruction of Nazi tyranny" and promised to support "the right of all peoples to choose the form of government under which they will live."

December 7: Japan bombs Pearl Harbor.

December 11: Germany declares war on the U.S.

December 22: Churchill comes to Washington D.C. FDR decides to fight in the European theater before fighting Japan.

1945

May 1945: Germany surrenders to the Allies.

Table of Contents

List of Photographs

Photograph and Image Credits

Photographs and images that appear on the title page and on pages 12, 13, 13, 18, 22, 25, 26, 27, 29, 31, 85, 93 and 101
 © ANNE FRANK Fonds, Basel/Switzerland
 ©ANNE FRANK Fonds, Basel/ Anne Frank Stichting, Amsterdam

Photographs and images that appear on the title page and on pages 14, 18, 21, 52, 54, 57, 58, 59, 63 and 99
 Courtesy: Straus Historical Society, Smithtown, NY

Images that appear on pages 16 and 17
 Courtesy: UAH StudA Frank, Otto (1908)
 UAH StudA Straus, Nathan (1908)
 Heidelberg University, Heidelburg, Germany

Images that appear on pages 70, 71, 74, 85, 88 and 94
 Courtesy: Yivo: Institute for Jewish Research (New York), Collection of the Hebrew Immigrant Aid Society (HIAS), Record Group 245, Otto Frank case file.

Letter Reprint Credits

Permission to quote from the Otto Frank and Nathan Straus Jr. letters found in YIVO's Archives was granted by:

Hebrew Immigrant Aid Society (HIAS), Valery Bazarov, HIAS Director Location and Family History

YIVO Institute for Jewish Research (New York), Collection of the Hebrew Immigrant Aid Society (HIAS), Record Group 245, Otto Frank case file.

Permission to quote from the Otto Frank and Nathan Straus Jr. letters found in ANNE FRANK-Fonds was granted by:

©Anne Frank FONDS, Basel/Anne Frank Stichting, Amsterdam

Permission to quote from the Otto Frank and Nathan Straus Jr. letters found in the Straus Historical Society's Archives was granted by:

Straus Historical Society, Inc., Smithtown, NY

Acknowledgements

No author writes a book in isolation. Many people, and in this case institutions, contributed to my effort. I could not write nor publish *For the Sake of the Children* without their support.

As executive director of the Straus Historical Society, part of my work is researching and documenting the lives of the many members of the Straus family. I had long known of the relationship between Otto Frank and Nathan Straus Jr. and had contributed information to many authors who were writing their own books about Otto Frank's life and about the relationship between the two friends. Thank you to all those authors who came before me and laid the groundwork upon which I was able to draw both information and inspiration.

When a cache of letters between Otto Frank and Nathan Straus Jr. was accidentally found in YIVO's archives by volunteer Estelle Guzik, past president of the Jewish Genealogical Society of New York, she noticed that names and dates were missing from the file folder. Part of her job was to document the information in each file. It was then that she realized whose file it was and its importance. She notified Carl Rheins, former executive director of YIVO. Once all the paperwork was complete and the legal provenance established, Carl Rheins invited me to the declassification ceremony for the file's contents and gave me a copy of the complete set of letters. Thank you Carl for thinking of me. (YIVO, Institute of Jewish Research, 15 West 16 Street, New York, NY 10011). And thank you Estelle for your volunteer work and for your diligence.

I wrote an article about the newly discovered letters between Otto Frank and Nathan Straus Jr. for the August 2007 issue of the Straus Historical Society's semiannual newsletter, http://www.straushistoricalsociety.org/uploads/1230925409nwsltr807.pdf Thanks must go to the board of directors of the Straus Historical Society for giving me the freedom to pursue any avenue of research that piques my interest and for their continued support of me and of my work. (Straus Historical Society, Inc., Post Office Box 416, Smithtown, NY 11787-0416)

I sent a copy of the August 2007 SHS newsletter to Buddy Elias, Anne Frank's cousin and head of ANNE FRANK-Fonds. We have been corresponding for years, sharing information about the relationship of Otto Frank and Nathan Straus Jr. As a result of my article, I was contacted by John D. Goldsmith, vice president of ANNE FRANK-Fonds, at the request of Buddy Elias and fully supported by the other members of their Board. John invited me to submit a proposal for a project relating to the letters and the relationship of the two men. And so, this book began with a grant from ANNE FRANK-Fonds. Thank you Buddy Elias, John D. Goldsmith and the members of the board of ANNE FRANK-Fonds, Basel/Switzerland for your faith in me and for your patience. (www.annefrank.ch)

There could be no way for me to present the letters in a more meaningful and powerful manner than to provide quotes from them. Thank you to director Valery Bazarov of HIAS (Hebrew Immigrant Aid Society, 333 Seventh Avenue, 16th Floor, New York, NY 10001-5019) for permission to quote extensively from the letters.

Having never written a book of this nature before, I found the journey quite daunting. I was comfortable doing the research, and even with the writing. Even though it was my idea to write this book, once I'd made the commitment, getting this book from the concept to the manuscript and then to publication completely overwhelmed me. Adaire J. Klein, Director of Library and Archival Services at Simon Wiesenthal Center (1399 South Roxbury Drive, Los Angeles, CA 90035-4709) introduced me to other authors, invited me to speak about my project at the Center and provided the push I needed to bring my book to publication. Thank you Adaire.

Dr. Andreas J. Schwab of Beaconsfield, Quebec did several translations from German. He also has amazing research skills. Andreas always provides the context of the translations he completes and then goes beyond that to enrich my understanding of their historical significance. Thank you Andreas. I am in your debt.

Thank you to the many people who have heard my talk about this project and given me the encouragement I needed to publish *For the Sake of the Children*. Your support is greatly appreciated.

Thank you to my wonderful husband Frank who has given me guidance, support, patience and love during my many emotional hours researching and writing *For the Sake of the Children*. Thank you for your amazing design for the cover of *For the Sake of the Children*. I could not have completed this book without his almost encyclopedic knowledge of the period, his exceptional Photoshop skills and his unwavering faith in my ability.

Preface

In 1959 a powerful movie opened in New York City. It was *The Diary of Anne Frank*. I remember seeing it with a group of my friends, all of us young teenagers. As Anne and her family were led away from their hiding place in the attic at Prinsengracht 263, I sobbed uncontrollably. I thought, "Why didn't they leave Amsterdam when they had the chance? Why didn't they get out?"

These questions have remained with me for more than fifty years.

Now I am grown and have had the opportunity to work at several interesting careers. For the past twenty two years I've been the historian for the Lazarus Straus family from Otterberg, Germany. I didn't know until recently that my fifty four year old question would be answered because of my present profession, historian for the Straus family.

The New York Times and *Time Magazine* articles during January and early February 2007 tell of the discovery of a file containing letters written in 1941 between Otto Frank and Nathan Straus, Jr. These letters reveal, for the first time, that Otto Frank, the father of Anne Frank, recognized the danger his family faced and was anxious to leave Amsterdam.

Otto Frank's correspondent, Nathan Straus Jr., was Otto's roommate at Heidelberg University. They remained lifelong friends. In 1941, when these letters were written, Nathan Straus Jr. was the director of the United States Housing Authority in President Franklin Delano Roosevelt's administration. He had the ear of the president and was a great friend of FDR's wife Eleanor.

The letters between Otto Frank and Nathan Straus Jr. were released to the public when New York-based YIVO Institute for Jewish Research held their declassification ceremony on February 14, 2007. They document Otto Frank's desperate but futile effort to save his family and Nathan Straus, Jr.'s desire to help. But the tightening restrictions of the U.S. State Department, along with deteriorating conditions in Europe, prevented anyone, even those with powerful connections and money, from securing the necessary documents to allow the Frank family to immigrate.

After reviewing these letters, it appears that timing and luck were more important than connections.

It will be necessary to present a brief biographical sketch of each of these men. For only within the context of their own personal history can one understand the forces that drove each man to make the decisions that so dramatically affected the lives of the Frank family.

This is **not** a history book about World War II. The author expects that the reader already knows the basic facts regarding the war as it manifested itself in the European theater. Only the information that is relevant, that puts the lives of Otto Frank and his family, and Nathan Straus Jr. and his family, into historical context will be expanded upon.

And this is **not** a book about Anne Frank. Many books have been written about Anne and about her diary. These were consulted for factual information about the events leading up to Frank's family going into hiding at Prinsengracht 263. But her story will not be retold here, nor will their months of hiding in the attic be retold. This books relates the events that took place more than a year before the Frank family went into hiding.

This **is** a book about Anne Frank's father, Otto Frank, his relationship with Nathan Straus jr., the recently discovered letters between them, and the information that has come to light because of their discovery. The letters put a whole new light on a subject that was once quite baffling: why Otto Frank didn't try to get his family out of Holland. They bring us new understanding of just how hard Otto Frank tried to get his family to safety and the forces that conspired against the efforts of not only Otto Frank, but his friend Nathan Straus Jr., Edith Hollander Frank's brothers Walter and Julius Hollander and several agencies within the United States.

We have long known of the relationship between Otto Frank and Nathan Straus, Jr. You will learn more about this as you read through my book. The newly discovered letters expand our knowledge about that relationship and give us greater insight into this tragic era in history.

Chapter One - December 11, 1941

Dates involved with World War II can be thought of as those of significance to many people and those that aren't noted at all.

Americans won't forget December 7, 1941, the day that America was thrust into war with the Japanese after the bombing of Pearl Harbor in Hawaii nor will they forget June 6, 1944, the day the liberation of Western Europe was started.

But December 11, 1941 does not stir any specific memories for most people. Nor does it evoke the emotional response elicited by December 7, 1941 or June 6, 1944.

On December 11, 1941 the war with Japan was 4 days old. America was trying to understand the treachery at Pearl Harbor and the debacle evolving in the Philippines, Guam and Wake Island. President Roosevelt was busy allaying America's fears and organizing a massive response to the Japanese attack.

December 11, was the day that Germany and Italy made it official. They declared war on the United States of America.

December 11, 1941 was the day that sealed the fate of aspiring refugees from Nazi persecution. It was the day that occupied Europe developed a malignant fog. And Otto Frank and his family disappeared. They had not yet gone into hiding in the attic at Prinsengracht 263. But all communication with their family and friends in America was cut off.

Chapter Two – Otto and Charley

Otto Frank, Anne Frank's father, was a man of ideals and strong principles. He had unshakable faith in man's humanity. He believed that goodness and patriotism were traits common to all men and that an evolved society would honor those traits.

When these beliefs were shattered by the Nazi atrocities, he hoped that escape was possible. But even with connections at the highest level of the American government, that escape proved elusive.

Otto Frank began his studies at Heidelberg University in 1908. He was interested in economics. His college roommate was Charles Webster Straus (later known as Nathan Straus Jr.). Both men planned to complete their education and join their family's business. Otto Frank's father, Michael Frank, owned Michael M. Frank Bank in Frankfurt, Germany. Charles Webster Straus' father, Nathan Straus, was the owner, with his brother Isidor, of Macy's Department Store in New York City.

Neither young man imagined the importance of their budding relationship. Nor could either foresee how the changing political climate in Europe would affect them. After all, December 11, 1941 was 33 years in the future.

Otto Heinrich Frank was born May 12, 1889 in Frankfurt, the second son of Michael Frank. Michael was the owner of a bank specializing in foreign currency exchange. Otto's older brother Robert was born in 1886. Brother Herbert was born in 1891 and their sister Helene (Leni) joined the family in 1893.

Theirs was a life of culture and privilege. The children attended private preparatory schools. They studied languages, learned to play instruments, rode horses and went to the opera. Although they strongly identified with their Jewish co-religionists, they did not attend services at the synagogue. Their religion was simply another aspect of their identity.

The Frank children: Robert, Otto,
Herbert and Helene (Leni) - about 1896

Otto was popular with his classmates. He was outgoing and liberal. His parents taught him that tolerance was important. In the early twentieth century Germany's prominent Jews considered themselves Germans before thinking about their Jewish identity. This led to huge problems in 1933 when Hitler came into power. But that was later. In Otto's youth, and throughout the First World War, the Frank family enjoyed full German citizenship and all of its privileges.

Otto loved to travel. During the Easter school break in 1907 he went to Spain. After receiving his graduate certificate from Lessing Gymnasium in 1908, (Europe's version of high school), he spent his summer vacation in England. His travels were finally curtailed once it became impossible because of the war.

Otto Frank - 10 years old

The home of the Michael Frank family in Frankfurt

In 1908 Otto began taking classes at Heidelberg University. There he met Charles Webster Straus. The two quickly developed a friendship. They were both sons of prominent German Jewish families. The Straus and Frank families were on parallel paths, a continent apart.

Along with being co-owner of R. H. Macy & Company with his older brother Isidor, Nathan Straus was Macy's outside buyer. He made regular trips to Europe. In 1875, on one of his European trips, he met Lina Gutherz. Within six weeks they were married. Their son Charles Webster Straus was born the same month and year as Otto Frank. His birth date was May 27, 1889. (Adolf Hitler was born April 20, 1889.)

The Straus family: Charles Webster, Lina, Nathan,
Hugh Grant and Sissie in their New York City apartment

Between 1876 and 1890 Nathan and Lina had six children. Two of their children died when they were young causing Nathan to ponder the problem of childhood mortality. He noticed that a cow on their farm was sick with tuberculosis, a common bovine disease at that time. He wondered if the disease could spread from the cow's milk to infect children. As a result, Nathan began to research how milk could be purified. He'd met Louis Pasteur during one of his previous trips to Europe and became convinced that pasteurization was the solution.

In 1892 Nathan opened the first pasteurization laboratory for milk purification. It was located in New York City. He set up milk depots around the city where poor families could receive free or inexpensive clean milk to give to their children. He dramatically reduced the death rate of the city's children because of this process of purifying their milk. Nathan offered to build and pay for a pasteurization laboratory in any city in the United States or anywhere in the world if they would send doctors to learn the process.

In 1908 Nathan and Lina were in Heidelberg, Germany where the Nathan Straus Pasteurization Laboratory was located at Grabengasse No. 8 across the plaza from the university. They were traveling around Europe trying to convince municipalities and health care professionals of the importance of pasteurization.

When they left for Europe their son Charles Webster Straus (who later changed his name to Nathan Straus, Jr.), was enrolled at Princeton University in New Jersey. In an unpublished autobiography Nathan, Jr. described his dissatisfaction with the university program. He decided to attend Heidelberg University where Otto Frank became his college roommate.

Carol Ann Lee, in her book *The Hidden Life of Otto Frank*, quoted from a letter written by Nathan Straus Jr. to Eleanor Roosevelt in 1957. He described meeting Otto Frank through members of his wife's family (Helen Sachs Straus) from Mannheim who "knew the Frank family intimately." Charley (Nathan Jr.) and Otto attended classes together and spent many evenings with Charley's parents. He said Otto was his closest friend during his time in Heidelberg and that his parents liked Otto the best of all his friends.

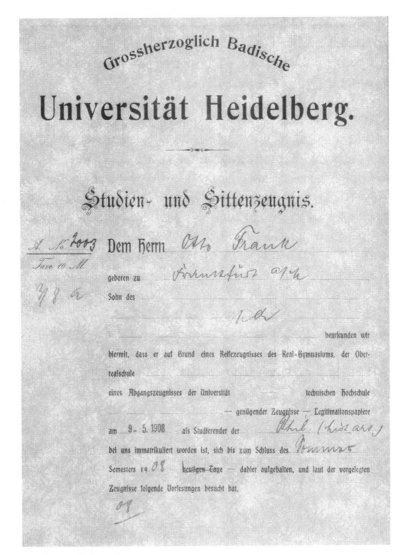

Grand-Ducal Baden University of Heidleberg
Certificate of Studies and Conduct
A. Number 2003
Fee 10 Marks
We attest herewith that Mr. Otto Frank
born at Frankfurt a/M (am Main)
son of n.a.
based on sufficient transcripts and legitimate papers was registered on May 9, 1908 as a student of Philosophy, department of History, remained until the end of the summer semester 1908 and, according to the credit certificates presented, has attended the following courses, 08

16

Universität Heidelberg.

Studien- und Sittenzeugnis.

A. No. 2569
Taxe 10 M

Dem Herrn *Nathan Straus*

geboren zu *New-York*

Sohn des

beurkunden wir

hiermit, dass er auf Grund eines Reifezeugnisses des Real-Gymnasiums, der Ober-

realschule

eines Abgangszeugnisses der Universität   technischen Hochschule

— genügender Zeugnisse ₰ Legitimationspapiere

am *2. 11. 1907* als Studierender der *Philosophie*

bei uns immatrikuliert worden ist, sich bis zum Schluss des *Sommer*

Semesters 19 *08* — heutigen Tage — daher aufgehalten, und laut der vor-

gelegten Zeugnisse folgende Vorlesungen besucht hat.

07/8, 08

Grand-Ducal Baden University of Heidelberg
Certificate of Studies and Conduct
A. Number 2569
Fee 10 Marks
We attest herewith that Mr. Nathan Straus
born in New York
son of n.a.
based on sufficient transcripts and legitimate papers was registered on November 11, 1907 as a student of Philosophy, remained until the end of the summer semester 1908 and, according to the credit certificates presented, has attended the following courses, 07/8, 08 (August 7, 1908)

Left: Otto Frank
Below: Charles Webster
Straus - 1907
about the time of their
attendance at Heidelburg
University

Otto, whose family lived in Frankfurt, attended Heidelberg University during the summer semester of 1908 that started on April 27. His admission paper states that he studied "Philosophy, Department of History." According to the Anne Frank Foundation website, he studied Economics. In any case, Otto found the courses contained too much theory. He returned to Frankfurt where he began working at his father's bank. He had every expectation of remaining there throughout his career and making important contributions to its successful continuation.

Charley studied Philosophy at the university for two semesters; winter 1907/1908 and summer 1908. Nathan, Lina, Nathan Jr. and Nathan's brother, H. Grant Straus, sailed to New York aboard the "Cedric," arriving September 4, 1908. Charley (Nathan Jr.) returned to Princeton after the completion of his two semesters in Heidelberg.

In 1909, Nathan Straus, at the urging of his son, invited Otto Frank to New York to work at Macy's. Nathan told his son that if Otto decided to stay at Macy's after a year's experience, a good future awaited him there.

Otto's father Michael encouraged the move because he felt it would be a good opportunity for his son to practice his English and to learn about foreign commerce. Michael Frank expected that his son would return to Frankfurt and join the family's banking business after his sojourn in the United States. It would be advantageous for Otto to be fluent in English and familiar with America's banking regulations when he returned to his family's bank at home in Germany.

Otto sailed from Bremen, Germany on September 7, 1909 aboard the "Kaiser Wilhelm der Grosse." The manifest lists him as a 20 year old merchant last living with his father, Michael M. Frank in Frankfurt. The ship arrived in New York on September 14th, just ten days after Nathan Jr.'s family arrived back in New York.

Otto wrote to his sister Leni from New York on December 29, 1909. He explained that he had a "good relationship with Charlie" and that he was meeting young women. He wrote, "You cannot imagine how often I think of you and how I feel here. It seems I don't know how lucky I am to live in this house and feel so at home." [1]

After gaining experience working at Macy's, Otto determined that merchandising was not for him. With the complete understanding and support of the Straus family, he left the firm to find employment with a U.S. bank.

His letter to Leni of August 29, 1910 describes his search for a new apartment and his happiness at finding "an adequate room" on West 71st Street, which was much closer to the Strauses West 72nd Street home. Otto anticipated learning about the American financial system and enjoying the social benefits he was gaining because of his friendship with the Strauses.

At the age of twenty-one Charles Webster Straus legally changed his name to Nathan Straus Jr. He knew that he did not want to follow in the family business, merchandising. He was planning to enter the world of publishing but also contemplated a future political career.

It is understandable that he wanted to bank on the much more recognized name of his father, Nathan Straus. He gave everyone three months to learn to call him Nathan. Almost everyone made the switch. But not everyone. His sister-in-law, Flora Stieglitz Straus, Hugh Grant's wife, took great delight in calling him Charley, just to incite him. Otto Frank also continued to call his friend Charley and was, perhaps, the only one who could get away with it without inciting his friend's anger.

Macy's at Herald Square, New York City - 1904

Otto Frank in uniform during World War I

Chapter Three – Otto in Europe

During 1909 and 1910, while he was living in the United States, Otto made several trips back to Germany but returned to New York where he continued working at Macy's and then in a New York bank. His social life revolved around the Straus family. They were, after all, the people who invited him to the United States and who had the contacts and influence to open doors to future employment as well as to society.

In 1909 Otto's father Michael died. Otto, who had a strong sense of responsibility to his family, considered returning to Europe at that time to help with the family's bank. But he was encouraged by his family to stay in the United States and to continue learning. However, feeling the pull of responsibility, by mid 1911, Otto returned home. He took an office job with a metal engineering firm in Dusseldorf where he felt he could continue to learn the economics of business and be close to his family in Frankfurt.

His enjoyment of traveling continued. He regularly visited his brother Herbert and his cousin Milly Stanfield. Both were living in London. He also spent time with family members in Switzerland in 1912.

In early 1914 Europe was preparing for war. Anti-Semitism was on the rise. Jewish men were finding it difficult to enroll in German military academies but they were expected to serve in the military. Otto's Dusseldorf employers loaned Otto to a company that did important war work which enabled him to avoid active military service.

Despite this, in 1915 he was called to service as was his brother Robert. Otto was attached to an infantry unit as a range-finder. He entered the war as a private but became one of the few Jewish officers, a lieutenant, by the end of the war. Although his letters to sister Leni remained upbeat, it appears that Otto actually felt the depression of serving under difficult circumstances. Otto's sense of responsibility, not only toward his family but also toward his country, and his identification as a "true" German, allowed him to serve with pride to help his country's war effort.

The war ended in November 1918 but Otto didn't return home immediately. He'd made a promise to a Belgian family that, once the war was over, he would return the two horses his unit appropriated during the war. After returning the horses it took him three weeks to walk back home. By this example alone one can see that Otto Frank was a man of character.

The vast shortages of supplies and food in Germany continued after the war. Jews became easy scapegoats for the frustration and deprivation felt by the general population. Adding to this, the Frank's family bank was in trouble due to bad investments in war bonds that were now worthless. Otto felt it was necessary to take over the running of the bank and other family owned businesses, one of which made cough and cold lozenges.

Anti-Semitism was on the rise in the 1920s but Otto was far more worried about his family's business troubles than of the dangerous political situation that was developing. The business problems led Otto and his brother-in-law Erich Elias, Leni's husband, to open a branch of the Michael M. Frank & Sons Bank in Amsterdam in late 1923. The following year the firm hired Johannes Kleiman. This turned out to be a very fortunate association as Kleiman was one of the people who protected Otto's family when they were in hiding. The Amsterdam bank failed at the end of 1924 but it took four years for the final dissolution.

His family in debt, Otto returned to Frankfurt from Amsterdam in early 1925. He was still trying to be forward looking, trying to figure out how to make a living and to have a family before he became too old. In April he announced his engagement to Edith Hollander of Aachen, Germany.

Edith, born in 1900, was the daughter of Abraham and Rosa Hollander. Edith was the youngest child in the family, joining siblings Julius, Walter, and Bettina. When she married, Edith's family provided a substantial dowry, as was the custom at that time. Their marriage provided Otto with the money he needed to keep his businesses solvent and the wife who would provide him the family he desired. Although Otto Frank was devoted to his wife, it has been suggested that theirs was not a love match.

Edith Hollander - circa 1925

Edith was an observant Jew who kept a kosher home, attended synagogue on the Sabbath and observed all the Jewish holidays. Although Otto didn't participate in his wife's observance, he had no problem with her devotion.

In February 1926 daughter Margot was born. At the time, Otto and Edith were living in his mother's house in Frankfurt along with his sister Leni, her husband Erich Elias and their two children. Stephan and Buddy. Otto and Edith longed for a home of their own. (Note: Buddy Elias, Otto Frank's nephew, is the chairman of the board of ANNE FRANK-Fonds, Basel, Switzerland.)

Otto Frank and Edith Hollander
May 12, 1925

Conditions for Jews in Germany were worsening when Otto and his family moved away from the center of Frankfurt into smaller accommodations. It was a non-Jewish neighborhood but they had their own home.

Although it was clear from the beginning that their landlord, Otto Koenitzer, was anti-Semitic, their stay in this house was mostly pleasant. Koenitzer believed that Jews should not be full-fledged German citizens. And, although he thought all Jews were rich and took jobs away from deserving Germans, he was realistic enough to see that the Franks paid their rent on time and were, therefore, good tenants. The Frank's other neighbors were open-minded people who didn't care that the Franks were Jewish. They all got along well.

In the late 1920's Otto was a liberal who "voted for the German Democratic Party, which stood for progress and a growth-oriented economy based on private enterprise, social justice, tolerance, compassion, and individualism."[2]

In June 1928 Otto and Edith enjoyed a vacation with Nathan Straus Jr. and his family at a villa in Sils-Maria, in the Upper Engandine valley of Switzerland. Otto's sister and her family lived in this area and it's possible that her family vacationed with them as well.

Nathan Straus Jr. with his four sons: Nathan III, Barnard Sachs, Irving Lehman and R. Peter Straus - 1928 in Sils-Maria, Switzerland

The following year Otto and Edith Frank's second daughter, Annelies Marie, was born on June 12, 1929. Annelies was known as Anne throughout her short life.

Just four short months later the New York Stock Exchange crashed, throwing world markets into crisis. The Frank's bank lost 90% of its business. Otto struggled to keep open the firm that had been his family's for so many years. He felt it was his obligation.

Jews became easy scapegoats as conditions worsened in Germany. Incidents of anti-Semitism increased. Jews were banned from many professions. Otto was continually urged to leave Germany by friends, family members and business associates. His sister Leni and brother-in-law Erich Elias and their family lived in Basel, Switzerland where they opened a branch of Opekta, a company that made pectin and gelling agents for jam preparation.

Otto, like many others, felt he was a German first, and because he fought for Germany in World War I, would not face discrimination. We now know this was not the case. The Aryanization of Germany dictated that many Germans were excluded from the privileges of their countrymen.

Cousin Milly Stanfield, who visited the Franks from London, found the conditions in Germany impossible. Although Otto told her that he didn't like what was happening, he maintained an optimistic view and planned to remain in Germany hoping that the danger would soon pass.

But slowly, over the next few years, conditions worsened.

In April 1932 Otto wrote to his sister Leni in Basel, "There is no telling where we're heading. The only bright spot is the children, who are sweet and take my mind off our troubles."[3]

At the end of 1932, after the complete failure of the Frank's family bank and a law suit brought against Otto's brother Herbert, the bank's manager, Otto understood that the family could no longer stay in their home. They moved even further from the center of the city. Otto finally acknowledged that this move was only temporary. He was beginning to realize that they would have to leave Germany as the Nazi Party was gaining too much support.

Margot, Otto and
Anne Frank
about 1932

In January 1933 Hitler was elected chancellor promising the German people dominance in international business affairs and a new era of national pride. There was a nationwide boycott of Jewish businesses and new laws were enacted to prevent Jews from participating in business or social life in Germany. Jews who, in the past, felt they were Germans and would not face active discrimination, realized they were wrong.

December 11, 1941 was still eight years in the future.

The German policy at that time was to force Jews to leave. They has not yet conceived of "The Final Solution." Many Germans Jews did leave but most felt as Otto did, that their German nationality took precedence over their religion. And, because their families had lived in Germany for centuries, and because they had successful businesses, they would not be harmed or deprived of their livelihood. It wasn't long before they learned a very hard lesson and were proved wrong.

The United States government, led by President Franklin Delano Roosevelt, began negotiations with the German government in an effort to allow its citizens to emigrate but also to take their possessions with them. The Germans were all too happy to have the Jews leave but they wanted their property to remain in Germany. For families like the Franks, who had been in Germany for centuries, and whose businesses were successful, leaving without their possessions seemed unthinkable.

By 1933 Otto and Edith, both with German roots going back centuries, decided they could no longer live in a country where anti-Semitism was rampant. Otto had tried to establish a business in Amsterdam before and failed. Now he knew he had no choice but to try again. He wrote, "The world around me has collapsed. When most of the people of any country turned into hordes of nationalist, cruel anti-Semitic criminals, I had to face the consequences, and although this hurt me deeply I realized that Germany was not the world and I left forever."[4]

Holland seemed like a natural choice for his family's immigration. It had, for centuries, been a place of refuge for the persecuted like the French Huguenots and the English Puritans. Now it was becoming what seemed like a safe haven for the Jews of Europe.

Otto moved to Amsterdam in August 1933 while his wife and daughters stayed near the Belgium border in Aachen where the Hollanders lived. Edith and daughter Margot joined him in December and Anne followed with her maternal grandmother in February 1934.

The family settled into their new apartment at Merwedeplein 37 in a section that was rapidly receiving immigrants from all over Europe. Many of these immigrants were forced to leave their homeland for political or economic reasons, not because they were Jewish. The Reich Representatives of the Jews in Germany estimated that by the end of 1933 approximately 63,000 Jews had emigrated. But only 32 percent of the residents in the area around Merwedeplein were Jewish. The people living there, no matter what their nationality or religion, had an immediate connection because almost all of them had been transplanted from their homes and were starting over in a new country.

A friend and Anne playing on the street,
Merwedeplein, in Amsterdam

With the help of a loan from his brother-in-law Erich Elias, who was the manager of the Swiss branch of Opekta, Otto opened the Dutch branch of Opekta. It was a business that sold pectin for making jams.

Otto and Edith were not the only ones in their families leaving Germany. Otto's brother Robert and his wife moved to London where they became art dealers. His brother Herbert was already living in France, having moved there to avoid further prosecution as a result of the lawsuit against the Frank family's bank. Otto's mother Alice moved to Basel, Switzerland to be with her daughter Leni and her family. Edith's brothers Walter and Julius soon found that they, too, were unable to stay in Germany.

For centuries the Netherlands was a center for Jewish immigration. The growing power of the Nazi Party and the deteriorating conditions in Europe caused a mass emigration of Jews into the Netherlands by 1933. A second wave came in 1935 after the enactment of the Nuremberg Laws stripped Jews of their citizenship and prohibited them from sexual relationships or marriage to non-Jews.

After Kristallnacht (Crystal Night, the Night of Broken Glass) in 1938, a third migration flooded the country with people trying to find a place where they could be safe. Many found that their nationality, being German, rather than their religion, being Jewish, acted against them. There was fear, even among Dutch Jews, that the masses arriving would stimulate anti-Semitism in the Netherlands.

Otto Frank needed to make a living without attracting attention. He advised his family to speak Dutch whenever they were outside their home. The girls, who quickly picked up the language, were enrolled in the local Montessori school. Edith took care of the household but found the transition difficult. Otto, Margot and Anne spent most of the day outside of their home and with other people. They rapidly learned to converse in Dutch but Edith, who spent most of her day at home, found the language challenging. She felt isolated.

Although economic conditions were difficult, Otto managed to build his branch of Opekta. He moved to larger quarters and hired a small staff. Work was much harder than it had been in Germany. He found the hours long. He spent much of his time traveling around Holland trying to drum up business. In a letter to his former neighbor, Gertrud Naumann, who still lived in Frankfurt, he explained that he worked continuously all-day and only came home in the evening. This was unlike his workday in Frankfurt where he came home at noon, had lunch with his family and rested before returning to work.

It was still possible for a Jew to travel in Europe. In June of 1935 Anne and her Hollander grandmother, visited their family in Switzerland. At the end of the year Otto and Margot visited the Elias family in Basel, Switzerland to celebrate their paternal grandmother's 70th birthday. During the summer of 1936 Edith, Margot and Anne went to Sils Maria in Switzerland, a trip Anne remembered fondly in a letter to her grandmother in Basel in 1941. Otto went to Germany on business in the summer of 1936. That was the last time he was able to do so.

Perhaps it was Otto's love for travel, or because he and Edith were trying desperately to shield their children from the deteriorating conditions around them, the family took many small trips to places like Middelkerke, a Belgian seaside resort. In March 1938 they toured the Dutch canals on a houseboat.

They also tried to provide entertainment at home as a way to keep their lives as normal as possible. Edith taught Margot and Anne to knit and sew. She also tried to interest them in religion; something that Margot found more interesting than Anne. It wasn't until the Nazi's occupation of Holland in 1940 forced the issue of religion upon the German Jews who were living in Amsterdam that the Franks began to see themselves as Jews. Until then their primary identification was German.

Edith Frank was the worrier of the family. After Hitler marched unopposed into the Rhineland in 1936 she may have encouraged Otto to look for work in England. When neighbors decided to move to the United States and asked Otto to join them, he responded that there was no need. Compared to the difficulties they'd experienced in Germany, Otto thought that life was restored to them in the Netherlands. The children were able to attend the public schools and he could work. They had started over and he felt free. He believed in the goodness of mankind and felt they should focus on that.

December 11, 1941 was still several years away.

Toward the end of 1937 Otto began looking for additional business. He could still move around parts of Europe unchallenged, making stops in Basel, Paris, London, Bristol and Luxembourg. His cousin Milly Stanfield encouraged him to reestablish himself in London but Otto was not anxious to uproot his family again. He wrote that he didn't know what to do about the girls. She later recalled that she urged Otto to send the children to her, letting him know that she would keep them safe. He responded, "Edith and I discussed your letter. We both feel we simply can't do it. We couldn't bear to part with the girls. They mean too much to us."[5]

Realizing that conditions were worsening and that his first obligation was to his family, Otto applied for immigration visas in Rotterdam for himself and his family in 1938. By 1939 the waiting list contained more than 300,000 names so he was not hopeful that he would succeed. He was a German living in the Netherlands and fell under the American quota for Germans.

By now Americans were becoming Xenophobic, afraid of foreigners and especially intolerant of anyone who was German. They worried that German spies would be sent to their country. They also worried that too many immigrants would mean fewer jobs for American citizens. Although immigration quotas were allowing some people in, those numbers were very small compared to the numbers of people who wanted to immigrate to the U.S.

The Frank family felt somewhat protected in neutral Netherlands. Otto and Edith tried to shield their daughters from discrimination. But as, even in Amsterdam, anti-Jewish regulations increased, their world became smaller.

In early November of 1938 counselor von Rath at the German Embassy in Paris was shot by a Jewish student. The Germans retaliated by unleashing a pogrom against the Jewish communities around Germany. They burned synagogues, homes, stores and books. They broke the windows of Jewish owned shops and killed or captured many Jews. The event became known as Kristallnacht, the Night of Broken Glass. As a result of this overt action against the Jewish people, their places of business and their houses of worship, thousands of Jews fled to the Netherlands, the last to escape before the borders were closed by war.

On November 12, 1938 Walter and Julius Hollander, Edith's brothers, were arrested in Aachen. They were among 248 men arrests from their town. This was part of the ongoing round up of Jews following Kristallnacht. Julius was quickly released because he was a wounded veteran of World War I.

Walter was not so lucky and was sent to Sachsenhausen Concentration Camp. At that time concentration camps were used to detain people, or as work camps. They did not become death camps until 1942. The men were held temporarily as a form of humiliation. They were made to feel isolated and powerless. The ultimate goal was to force them to emigrate.

Walter was told he would be released if he could prove he had a way to leave Germany. The brothers considered immigrating to the United States but needed an affidavit (a letter of support) from someone living there.

Walter was transferred to Zeeburg, a Dutch internment camp not far from Amsterdam. He was able to write to his family and was even given occasional leaves outside the camp. Author Melissa Mueller wrote in her book *Anne Frank, The Biography*, "On December 1, 1938, 'the Jew Walter Hollander,' was released from the 'state concentration camp Sachsenhausen' and ordered 'to notify the police of his place of residence immediately.' The message the camp administrator impressed on its prisoners upon their release was a threatening one. If a single one of you tells anyone on the outside what you have seen here, we'll find you and bring you back immediately, no matter where in the world you happen to be."[6]

Julius and his mother Rosa continued to live in Aachen where the family firm of B. Hollander remained open until closed by the Germans on January 29, 1939.

Julius and Walter received affidavits from a cousin, Ernst Hollander who was already in the U.S. He guaranteed them work and support once they arrived. In preparation for the departure of her sons, Edith's mother Rosa moved to Amsterdam where she lived out the rest of her life with her daughter Edith, Edith's husband Otto and their two daughters, Margot and Anne.

In an action that can only be called perversion, the Nazis, who made it impossible for the Hollander brothers to stay in Europe, and even demanded that they leave, required the Hollander brothers to deposit 2,070 Reichmarks into the account of the Reich Ministry of Commerce as a tax for their abandonment of the Reich.

Julius left for New York in April 1939. From there he moved to Massachusetts. Walter followed in December.

In the meantime, immigrants arriving in the Netherlands brought with them stories of the horrors they'd experienced. Many people, including Otto Frank, found it difficult to imagine that men could act in such a manner. Edith Frank believed it all. She remained unhappy with their situation but unable to find a solution.

Otto worked hard providing for his family at a time when it was becoming increasingly difficult to make a living. It was a little easier for him because he had the complete cooperation and support of his employees in Opekta. In October 1938 he opened a second firm that sold spices for food preparation, especially for the making of sausages. This company was called Handelsmaarschappij Pectacon N.V. Johannes Kleiman became the director. The first office of Pectacon was in Kleiman's apartment in Amsterdam.

Although, up until that time, there were few instances of anti-Semitism in the Netherlands, when it did occur, it was more likely to be verbal than physical. The Franks were more concerned about intolerance because they were Germans than because they were Jews. As more Jews arrived from around Europe, the Dutch began to worry that their own livelihood would be threatened. As a result, people began joining the Dutch Nazi Party, which became more powerful.

The situation in Europe was deteriorating. Austria had been annexed, then the Sudetanland fell, which led to the swallowing of Czechoslovakia. Germany and Russia signed a non-aggression pact in August 1939. In a secret deal, they agreed to the partition of Poland between them. On September 1, 1939 Germany invaded Poland. France and Great Britain gave Germany a chance to stop the invasion. When Germany refused to back down, France and Great Britain declared war.

Many people were forced to leave their countries. But they were the lucky ones. Once the borders of their homelands closed, conditions for the Jews got substantially worse. People had nowhere to go and felt powerless to help themselves. German decrees prevented non-Aryians from participating in community life. Jews were forbidden from practicing their profession, children could not attend public schools or visit parks and amusements. At least in the Netherlands, although there were hardships, there were few overt acts of aggression aimed at Jewish refugees.

On April 9, 1940 Norway and Denmark fell to the German Army.

The Dutch people became more and more alarmed as news of the horrifying treatment of the Jews reached them. Hitler continually reasserted that Holland, Belgium, Luxembourg and Switzerland would remain neutral. The Dutch people were skeptical but everyone wanted to believe this. Newspaper and radio accounts tried to placate the Dutch population.

Anne's sister Margot seemed aware of the political situation despite the protection of her parents. She wrote to her pen pal Betty Ann Wagner in Danville, Iowa in April of 1940 about her inability to visit her cousin in Basel. "We have to travel through Germany which we cannot do or through Belgium and France and that we cannot do either. It is war and no visas are given."[7]

One can rightfully ask why the Dutch didn't foresee the horrors to come. They suspected. They were warned. Then they grew skeptical.

For several months a German colonel leaked to the Dutch government that Hitler planned to invade Holland on a particular date. There were 29 leaks and each proved false. It's no wonder that no one in the Dutch government paid any attention to the information.

In May 1940 Germany invaded Luxembourg, France and the Netherlands. Blietzkrieg, meaning 'Lightning War,' refers to a fighting philosophy used by the Wehrmacht (German armed forces) of fast, highly mechanized, mobile attacks to quickly overwhelm the enemy and end a campaign quickly. This is what happened in May 1940. The Dutch city of Rotterdam was destroyed. The Dutch royal family ran, escaping to England. This shocked the Dutch people. They listened to their radios with horror as the Germans entered Amsterdam and, within five days of the invasion, Netherlands surrendered.

In May 1940, Reich Kommissar Arthur Seyss-Inquart took charge of the Netherlands. There was a German presence everywhere but life in Holland returned to an uneasy normalcy. The children still went to school and the people still worked. Seyss-Inquart issued statements designed to calm the local population and to assure them that nothing bad would happen during the occupation. But these, of course, were misleading communiqués and only meant to keep the people calm.

At first the Dutch people supported their Jewish neighbors. But, as conditions worsened, and repercussions for offering assistance to Jews became more violent, many Dutchmen withdrew their outward support. People stopped associating with Jews, which, of course, increased their isolation. This was just what the Germans wanted. Jews became increasingly powerless to help themselves.

For several years there had been restrictions placed on the Jews in occupied Europe. Now these restrictions reached Holland. Soon the restrictions included the closing of Jewish owned stores. Jews were prohibited from working at many occupations or serving in the Dutch government.

In October 1940, 14 months until December 11, 1941, additional restrictions were put in place preventing Jewish people from being on the street between the hours of midnight and four AM. No one could leave the country. Goods were becoming scarce. Every Jew over six years of age had to carry two identity cards, each displaying a photograph and marked with a large letter "J." They could no longer visit their Christian friends in their homes.

The Jews were not the only ones to face tightening restrictions. Limits were placed on what radio stations the people could listen to although most of the Dutch people still chose to listen to BBC in secret rather than the propaganda filled stations of the Dutch National Socialists.

By 1940 immigrants from Europe were flooding into the United States and Latin America. Fears of spies and subversives began to surface in those countries. By June, tightening visa control in the United States closed most of the options for would-be immigrants. Each had to show he was unlikely to engage in radical activities and have sufficient means to support himself in his new country. It was not enough to show he had a good reason to leave Europe. He also had to show that he had a good reason to enter the United States. People could be sponsored by relatives but they had to guarantee their successful assimilation by placing a large sum of money into a bank account in the immigrant's name.

By now Walter and Julius Hollander were struggling in the United States. Although they'd owned a family business in their native country and spoke English, they were unable to find meaningful work. Julius found a job at the Canton Japanning Company in Worcester, MA. This firm's business used a lacquering technique that made surfaces appear like that on furniture produced in Japan and other Asian countries.

Walter was employed by Jacob Hiatt at E. F. Dodge Paper Box Company in Leominster, MA.

Although the Hollander brother both worked in their own successful, prosperous family firm in Germany, their entry level jobs in the United States were of the kind that usually went to unskilled laborers.

Harry Levine, Julius' employer, and Jacob Hiatt, Walter's employer, found the Hollander brothers to be hard workers and developed sympathy when they learned about the family left behind in Amsterdam. Each man signed an affidavit of support; one for Margot and one for Anne in May 1941. This was remarkable because the Hollander brothers were relatively new employees and yet each of their employers, in signing the affidavit, agreed to assume financial responsibility for Margot and for Anne.

After Hitler invaded the Netherlands Otto thought it was too late to leave. The only possible escape route was by boat from the coastal cities near Rotterdam or Le Havre. Otto didn't have a car and he didn't think he could reach the coast. He thought it was too difficult to move his family of five: himself, a wife, two daughters and a mother-in-law who had cancer. He was worried that she wouldn't be accepted for a visa because of her illness. His sense of responsibility prevented him from leaving her behind.

By October 1940 Jews could no longer own businesses in Holland. Two of Otto Frank's trusted employees were named supervisory and managing directors of Opekta, making it appear that Aryans owned the firm. His employees agreed to this sham in order to keep Opekta operating and providing everyone with an income during these difficult times. Otto's other firm, Pectacon, was in the able hands of Johannes Kleiman.

Opekta and Pectacon moved to new quarters in the now famous Prinsengracht 263 in December 1940. There the offices were on the first floor while a warehouse occupied the ground floor. (The first floor is what Americans call the second floor.) The building included an annex. The floors could be entered from either side of the building since it was built into an incline. The annex remained largely unused and later became the hiding place for the Frank family once they felt it was necessary to disappear.

In spite of the new dangers and indignities, the Frank family tried to live as normal a life as possible under the circumstances. Otto felt this was important for his children. He hired an unemployed Berlin journalist to teach German literature to the girls and their friends. He later noted that this was difficult because so many people hated the Germans and everything German. But his deep affection and commitment for education overrode their discomfort.

The Jews of Holland were being strangled. Each new restriction was added slowly so as not to alarm them. These restrictions were printed in *Joodse Weekblad*, the Jewish weekly newspaper set up by the Jewish Council. While they added these restrictions, the Germans compiled a map showing where each Jew lived.

The borders around Holland were closed and goods were in short supply. Life was becoming more difficult for everyone.

Thinking they were helping the morale of the Dutch people, Winston Churchill, Prime Minister of the United Kingdom, and the Dutch Royal family in exile in England began making anti-German wireless broadcasts. People gathered around hidden radios to listen to their broadcasts.

Jews were forbidden to go to the movies so Otto rented films and a movie projector, holding screenings at home for his family and friends. Jewish musicians were not allowed to play in any orchestra paid for by the government. So evenings of music filled their apartments. As time progressed, laws were enacted prohibiting Jews from eating in restaurants and cafes. Then they were forbidden from visiting public parks, or zoos, or swimming in public pools. Their world was shrinking and they were powerless to prevent or stop it. Throughout all of this, Otto Frank worked hard to protect his daughters from the unpleasantness encroaching on their world.

By the winter of 1940-41 the Dutch people were frustrated and angered by the deprivations they had to endure. Although most people continued to support their Jewish neighbors, the Germans were starting to punish those who showed sympathy. Small fights began breaking out between the Dutch people and members of the Dutch Nazi Party (NSB).

In February 1941 fighting and political disturbances led to the sealing off of the Jewish quarter. Members of the Dutch Nazi Party (NSB) attended the funeral of one officer killed during a skirmish and used that occasion to stir up further sentiment against the Jews who they blamed for the incident.

To give the Jews a sense of control, the Joodse Raad Voor Amsterdam (Jewish Council for Amsterdam) was formed. Their function was to act as a liaison between the Jewish community and the Germans. The council was comprised of local Jewish citizens who cooperated with the Germans because they felt that resistance would lead to additional problems.

Shortly after the February 1941 fighting, several members of the Dutch Nazi Party were doused with ammonia when they entered a café where Jews congregated. The owners of the café and its customers were arrested and one of the owners was tortured and killed. This event led to more actions against the Jews.

Then, 425 Jewish men and boys were beaten, arrested and sent to Buchenwald and Mauthausen concentration camps. The Dutch people responded by calling a general strike to protest. It was disbanded after three days when the Germans and Dutch Nazis threatened them with severe punishment and martial law.

In March 1941 further restrictions were placed upon businesses that were once owned by Jews. It became necessary for Otto to report to the authorities that Pectacon, another of his businesses, was now owned by Johannes Kleiman and Anton Dunselman, a lawyer who was involved in Otto's business since 1920. The men were acting in name only, but their positions made it appear as if the firm was Aryan owned.

There were nine months remaining until December of 1941.

Accounts differ about what happened between the latter part of March and April of 1941. What is clear is that the situation for Otto Frank became desperate. He finally recognized that he and his family were no longer safe.

Otto Frank employed many people at his pectin and spice companies. Some were loyal to him and others were simply concerned about their own survival.

Otto later wrote that one employee, a man named Jansen, who built exhibition stands for his company, reported to the Bureau of National Security (BNV) that Otto had expressed the view that the war would go on for a long time and that Germany was having a tough time of it.

On April 18th, Tonny Ahlers, a young man with connections to the NSB, visited Otto Frank at his office. He told Otto that he was a courier between the NSB and the German SS. He questioned Otto about a letter written by Mr. Jansen to the BNV stating that Otto Frank made remarks that were insulting to the German Wehrmacht. After Otto gave Ahlers money to buy his silence, Ahlers gave Otto the letter. But he reminded Otto that he would remember what the letter contained and could use that information against him at any future date.

That meeting ripped any illusion of safety from Otto's life. He realized the blackmail would never stop and that his family was in danger. Finally, Otto became proactive.

On April 30, 1941 he wrote to his friend and former college roommate Nathan Straus, Jr. asking for assistance. Otto decided that he would have to emigrate with his family; to leave the Netherlands. "I would not ask if conditions here would not force me to do all I can in time to be able to avoid worse. ... It is for the sake of the children mainly that we have to care for. Our own fate is of less importance."[8]

Unknown to Otto there were seven and a half months left to act.

Otto Frank realized that, if he and his family were unable to leave Holland, they would need a safe place to hide. He began preparing the attic at Prinsengracht with the full support and cooperation of a few trusted staff at Opekta.

In her book, *The Hidden Life of Otto Frank*, Carol Ann Lee wrote, "Otto Frank had made a pact with the devil, but the price can scarcely be imagined. In working with his enemy, Otto hoped to protect not only his company but also himself and his family, for by then most Jewish people realized something of the immense danger that faced them. Throughout the war years, Otto was to all intents and purposes leading a double life. It was not just the business associations but the ever-present specter of Ahlers that haunted him – a man less than half his age who had saved his life but whose hold over him was profound. Jansen's terrible letter ensured that Otto remained in Ahler's debt. Ten years after the end of the war, in an unrelated matter, Otto wrote to his lawyer Myer Mermin that "no good comes from giving way to black-mail."[9]

Professor of History Richard Breitman at American University in Washington D.C. had an opportunity to review the letters between Otto Frank and Nathan Straus Jr. before they were declassified and released to the public. He wrote, "Otto Frank's efforts to move his family to the United States ... mirrored the experience of many thousands of German Jews. Frank's case was unusual only in that he tried hard very late - and enjoyed particularly good or fortunate American connections. Still he failed. The fact that Anne Frank was one of those who did not make it is a poignant reminder of what was lost."[10]

It is easy to wonder from today's prospective why Otto Frank and his family didn't leave Germany sooner. Or why they remained in the Netherlands while conditions were deteriorating. David Engel, the Greenberg Professor of Holocaust Studies at New York University compared the correspondence to a blind chess game where the rules kept changing. He states, "Understanding the situation of the Jews in the Netherlands under Nazi occupation, like understanding any aspect of the Holocaust, requires suspension of hindsight."[11]

Even the Nazi regime did not know that it would embark on a systematic program to exterminate the Jewish populations in their occupied territories. That wasn't decided until January 20,

1942 at the Wannsee Conference chaired by Reinhard Heydrich. At the conference, senior officials of the of the Nazi German regime defined what they called the "final solution to the Jewish question."

In 1941, while Jews were being deprived of their property and livelihood and becoming more socially isolated, they continued to live in relative security. Dutch Jews, in particular, were able to carry on their business throughout mid 1940 before increased restrictions were forced upon them.

By the fall of 1941 Jewish children were no longer allowed to attend secular schools. Anne and Margot transferred to the Jewish Lyceum, a school that was established by the occupying forces under the auspices of the Amsterdam Jewish Council. Their social life now revolved around that school and the other Jewish students.

Professor Engel wrote, "Raids on Amsterdam's Jewish quarter, initiated in February 1941, were quickly suspended in the wake of vigorous protests from Dutch organized labor: and in any event the Franks did not live in the Jewish quarter and were under no pressure to move there. In other words, in Otto Frank's case, neither the push nor the pull factors were as strong in 1940-41 as they had been in 1933. Hence he preferred what seemed to him like the nuisances that encumbered an otherwise comfortable life under Nazi occupation in the Netherlands to the insecurity of life as a double refugee in a new country, even if a new country could be found. ... There is little point in asking why Otto Frank did not wake up to the mortal danger facing his family sooner than he did: neither he nor anyone else could reasonably have predicted what would befall the Jews in the Netherlands beginning in 1942. His actions become intelligible only when viewed within the context of his individual experience, without benefit of hindsight."[12]

Chapter Four – Discovery of the Letters

The increasing number of immigrants to America at the end of the nineteenth century created a need for a mechanism to provide assistance for them. Although America is comprised almost entirely of an immigrant population, those who came earlier in the century were settled, employed for the most part, and had created thriving communities in their adopted homeland. The flood of new arrivals in the 1870s and 1880s threatened to overwhelm the cities where most of the immigrants were settling. New York and Philadelphia were most prominent.

A new organization, the Association for the Protection of Jewish Immigrants, was formed in Philadelphia at the end of 1881. It was guided by Jewish values and a knowledge of the difficulties that new immigrants faced. Among their services were: housing, employment, guidance about the new customs of their adopted country, and even relocation to the agricultural areas in the southern and western parts of the United States.

In the 1920s the name of the organization was changed to the Hebrew Immigrant Aid Society (HIAS). HIAS is still active today and is assisting immigrants who find their lives and freedom at risk. HIAS works to rescue, relocate and provide family reunification and resettlement to today's immigrants just as it did beginning in 1881.

Between 1948 and 1974 the files from the Hebrew Immigrant Aid Society (HIAS) and other organizations were transferred to the New York based YIVO Institute for Jewish Research which is part of the Center for Jewish History.

A file of letters, notes and telegrams that was not indexed was discovered in HIAS's archives by the Jewish Genealogical Society of New York's past president Estelle Guzik. She noticed that the names and dates were missing from the file.

When she opened the file to rectify the omission, she found the Frank family's records. The documents consist of personal correspondence between Otto Frank, Nathan Straus, Jr., Julius and Walter Hollander and governmental agencies. They date from April 1941 through December 1941 and continue in 1945, after the end of World War II. They shed new light on Otto Frank's attempts to rescue his family.

As these letters reveal, Otto Frank turned to his good friend, Nathan Straus, Jr., when desperation forced his hand. Although we'd known of this friendship, it wasn't until these additional letters were discovered that we realized the true closeness of these two men.

Nathan Straus Jr. was an excellent choice when Otto Frank realized the desperation of his situation. Straus was a senior member of FDR's government, the head of the United States Housing Administration. It is clear from the letters that they had continued their relationship throughout the years. Otto must have felt hope that if anyone could help him, it was his friend Nathan Straus Jr., a man with money and power, as well as influence and connections within the United States government.

The letters document Frank's desperate effort to save his family and Nathan Straus, Jr.'s desire to help. The tightening restrictions of the U.S. State Department, along with deteriorating conditions in Europe, prevented even those with powerful connections, and money, from securing the necessary documents that would allow the Frank family to immigrate.

Chapter Five - Nathan Straus Jr.

History tends to repeat itself and we seem unable to learn from the lessons of past. In difficult economic times a scapegoat is blamed for the troubles of the population.

This occurred in Germany when the Jews were blamed for the economic difficulties following World War I and also after the economic depression of 1929 that wreaked havoc across the industrial world.

Otto Frank's family was forced to leave its home and country almost one hundred years after Nathan Straus Jr.'s family left their home in Germany because of persecution.

Lazarus Straus, the father of Nathan Straus (Sr.), was born in Otterberg in southwestern Germany. Lazarus came from a family of merchants who bought and sold grains, cattle and wine. They were the most prominent family in their town.

After the death of his father in 1839 Lazarus Straus, the oldest of fourteen children, became the head of his family. Under his mature guidance, the family continued to prosper.

In 1848 a series of loosely coordinated protests and rebellions emphasized popular discontent with the traditional, largely autocratic political structure of the thirty-nine independent states of the German territory. They demonstrated the popular desire for increased political freedom, liberal state policies, democracy, nationalism, and freedom from censorship. The middle class elements were committed to liberal principles while the working class sought radical improvements to their working and living conditions.

Lazarus raised money for the cause but, after the revolution failed, the economic situation was difficult. Lazarus tried to financially help his younger siblings and their families who were in need, but declared bankruptcy in order to protect what was left of the family's fortune.

Then he learned that he was going to be called before the courts to explain his role in the revolution. Rather than risk further financial burdens and possible censure by the courts, and to protect what money was left for his family, Lazarus left Germany.

Just like Otto Frank many years later, Lazarus Straus decided he had no choice but to leave his native country in order to feel safe and to find a better life. He felt the responsibility to care for not only his wife and children, but to provide for his mother and siblings. The decision to leave Germany could not have been easy for Lazarus. We know it was not easy for Otto Frank.

Lazarus arrived in America in 1852 and was advised to go south to Georgia where there was economic opportunity. By 1854 he was sufficiently established to send for his family. They would be living in their new home in Talbotton, GA. There Lazarus had recently opened a dry goods store that sold cloth, clothing and necessities to the plantation families in the area. Most of his supplies came from the north, usually from Philadelphia. He made twice yearly trips there to restock his store.

Through hard work Lazarus established a comfortable life for his family. He was a respected member of the community. But the Civil War changed that. The southern population found it difficult, if not impossible, to obtain goods from the north. As conditions worsened, the people of Talbotton worried about how they would survive. They wanted someone to blame for their hardships and found their Jewish neighbors easy targets.

This was not much different from when the Jews of Germany were discriminated against almost a century later. There were difficult economic times and people wanted to find a place for the blame. In rural Georgia, there was a small Jewish population unlike the large German Jewish population of Otto Frank's era.

In Talbotton a proclamation was issued blaming the Jews for the lack of supplies, the high price of merchandise, and for generally making it more difficult to live. Lazarus Straus, who until that time had been treated as a valued member of the community, decided he could no longer live in Talbotton. The Jews were being blamed for the misfortune of others. Lazarus Straus was once again forced to leave his home. He packed his family and merchandise and moved 38 miles west to the larger city of Columbus.

As with the Holocaust, survival was awarded to the quick. Lazarus sensed the danger, acted, and his family survived. Otto Frank seemed to react after a period of denial and wishful thinking and his family paid the price.

By the end of the Civil War in 1865 the south was in ruins. General James H. Wilson burned Columbus, GA. He hadn't learned that the war was over. Out of desperation, Lazarus moved his family north, first to Philadelphia, where there was a large German Jewish population, and then to New York City.

Otto Frank moved his family further and further from Frankfurt as discrimination against Jews increased. He finally moved to Amsterdam as conditions became intolerable in Germany.

The Straus family was hard working and they prospered. Over time they established a china and crockery concession in the basement of Macy's Department Store. By 1894 they owned the entire store. Lazarus' second son Nathan, having too much energy to be contained in an office, traveled to Europe on buying trips and all over the United States opening up new markets.

On one of his European trips Nathan Straus met Lina Gutherz who lived in Ludwigshafen. Within six weeks they became engaged and then married in April 1875. Nathan and Lina had six children between 1876 and 1890: Jerome Nathan, Sara Gutherz, Sissie, Roland, Charles Webster and Hugh Grant. Sara and Roland died young. Their father believed that their deaths were caused by disease in milk. He began researching how to make the milk clean and found that pasteurization was the solution. In 1892 Nathan opened the first laboratory to pasteurize milk. He set up milk depots around New York City where poor families could receive free or inexpensive, clean milk for their children. By this alone he was able to dramatically reduce the death rate of the city's children.

Charles Webster (Nathan Jr.) Straus was born in the same month and year as Otto Frank, May 1889. Charlie was named to honor his father's friend and close business associate in family owned Macy's Department Store. Both Charlie Straus and Otto Frank were born into German Jewish families that had achieved financial success and prominence. Both families were assimilated, feeling close ties to their Jewish heritage but neither family observing Jewish ritual or regularly attending religious services. Although the children of both families were taught about their religion, their German identity seemed more important than their Jewish identity.

Charles Webster Straus
before 1907

The Straus family lived in a large New York City apartment at 27 West 72nd Street. They also had a summer house on Lower Saranac Lake in the New York's Adirondacks. Charlie was admitted to Collegiate School in New York City when he was eight years old. In his unpublished autobiography he wrote that it was then that his father, Nathan Straus, suggested that "that he would like to name me after him. I fell in enthusiastically with the idea. Mr. Webster meant absolutely nothing to me. So I was entered in the school as 'Nathan Straus, Jr.' – although for many years afterward practically everybody who called me by my first name called me "Charlie."[13] Although the seeds were planted, it wasn't until much later, in 1910, that Charles Webster Straus officially changed his name.

The family traveled abroad quite often and took their children with them. Charlie was frequently taken out of school so that he could accompany his parents.

Once again we find similarities in Otto Frank and Charlie's upbringing. Both grew up in families where tolerance was stressed. Both families were rooted in their Jewish religion and culture but neither was observant. Both boys enjoyed travel and spent many happy times traveling in their own countries and abroad. And both were exposed to the arts, music and culture.

The Straus family spent the winter of 1905 abroad. A tutor was hired who kept the children up on their studies. Although Charlie disliked this woman, he commented that she must have done a good job because he was well prepared when he entered Princeton University in the fall of 1906. After one year, and feeling dissatisfied with Princeton's program, Charlie transferred to Heidelberg University where he spent the following eighteen months. While at Heidelberg his roommate, Otto Frank, became one of his closest friends. Otto was studying economics in preparation for entering his own family's banking business.

At that time Charlie's parents were living in Heidelberg and had established the Nathan Straus Pasteurized Milk Laboratory across the street from the university. After three semesters abroad, Charlie returned to Princeton to complete his education.

In June 3, 1910, shortly after his graduation from Princeton, and upon reaching his twenty first birthday, Charles Webster Straus legally became Nathan Straus, Jr.

After graduating from Princeton, Nathan Jr.'s father intervened to help his son get a job with the *New York Globe*, a New York newspaper. Nathan Jr. wanted to learn the newspaper business by doing all of the jobs starting with compositing and reporting. But, after a short time, his father suffered a nervous breakdown and Nathan Jr. felt that, as the oldest son, it was his responsibility to hold his family's business affairs together. He went to work at Macy's when he was twenty-one years old knowing he was completely inexperienced and naïve about business.

Once again we can see that the experiences of Nathan Jr. and Otto Frank were similar. Otto Frank's father died in 1909 while Otto was in New York working at Macy's. He went back to Germany several times but returned to the United States. But after 1911 Otto went back to Europe one final time and remained there. The death of his father, and his feeling of re-

sponsibility toward his family and the family's bank in Frankfurt kept him there. Nathan Jr. also felt the responsibility to
carry on his father's business by going to work at Macy's when
his father was unable to work.

While Nathan Jr. was at Macy's, so were his older cousins, the
three sons of his uncle Isidor. They had all been working at Macy's since their graduation from Harvard, each rising to executive
positions that suited their experience and temperament. Jesse,
Percy and Herbert were truly the leaders of the firm.

**Just as Otto Frank was brought up with the expectation that
he would one day join the family's firm, Nathan Jr. expected
that he would one day become an executive at Macy's like his
older cousins.**

Shortly after Nathan's brother Isidor and Isidor's wife Ida died
in the Titanic disaster in 1912. Nathan Sr. withdrew from business and the sons of these two great men had a falling out. It
was decided that Macy's would remain in the hands of the three
brothers, Jesse, Percy and Herbert, who had been running it successfully for many years. The remaining family firms, Abraham
& Straus and L. Straus & Sons would now be owned by Nathan's
sons, Nathan Jr. and Hugh Grant. They were much younger than
their older cousins and did not have the merchandising exeri-
ence necessary to run the "world's largest department store." It
was a clean financial break but the two branches of the family
were no longer on speaking terms.

Nathan Straus Jr. realized that he was not interested in a career
in merchandising. After his brief stint at Macy's, he bought the
humorous periodical, *Puck* in 1913. He changed the focus of the
magazine to be like that of today's *New Yorker* magazine. It published articles about women's suffrage and financial and moral
aid to medical science. He led a campaign against the growing
militarism and chauvinism developing in America. And he introduced artwork from Europe and the U.S.

In 1914, while on a European trip with his sister Sissie and her husband, Judge Irving Lehman, the travelers became stranded in Munich when war was declared. They spent the next three weeks unable to access their letters of credit drawn on London banks. Finally, the Germans allowed a special train to take the thousands of stranded American tourists to Amsterdam, but only that far.

Nathan Jr. became stranded in the Netherlands during the First World War. Otto Frank was stranded in the Netherlands during the Second World War.

Once Nathan Jr., Sissie and Irving Lehman were in the Netherlands, a banker friend of Irving's arranged for them to be housed in a lovely Dutch seaside hotel in Scheveningen. The relief and subsequent gaiety felt by all Nathan Jr.'s fellow travelers can be appreciated. There, Nathan Jr. met the woman who would later become his wife, Helen Sachs, another stranded American.

The couple married on April 29, 1915. Helen's father, Dr. Barnard Sachs, was a prominent neurologist and psychiatrist of German Jewish descent. He is credited with discovering the early signs that indicate Tay-Sachs Disease. The Sachs family knew the Frank family in Mannheim and introduced the Strauses to the Franks many years before.

After a brief stay in Scheveningen, Nathan Jr. sailed for New York where he threw himself into the running of *Puck*. He adopted innovations that were mirrored later on by some of the larger publications. But, after four years and a growing circulation, he sold the magazine in 1917. He determined that it was still not making any money. He freely admitted in his autobiography that his lack of business experience and his unwillingness to settle down and actually run the publication were the prime factors in its failure.

Otto Frank had to deal with the failure of his family's bank. Nathan Jr. learned that it took more than money to keep his

business afloat. Both were confronted with the necessity of finding a new business.

Nathan Straus Jr. and Helen Sachs
wedding - 1915
Attendants are his brother and sister-in-
law Hugh Grant and Flora Stieglitz Straus

World War I was raging in Europe. Nathan Jr. obtained a commission in the United States Navy when the United States entered the war. Patriotism was high. Nathan Jr. wrote, "… it would have been a terrible blow not to have been able to do something in the war."[14] His nearsightedness should have kept him out of service. But his father interceded with the Secretary of the Navy who helped get him a commission. He was not sent to the European theater but was assigned a desk job in the cable censorship department.

Once again we see the similarities of Otto Frank and Nathan Straus Jr.'s experiences. Both men felt it was their patriotic duty to serve and were pulled from their jobs to serve their country during World War I. Of course the conditions for Otto Frank fighting in Europe were much more difficult.

Nathan Straus Jr. standing
Brother Hugh Grant Straus seated

After World War I we start to see Otto Frank's life take a different turn. From that point forward, although both men were hard workers who shared a love of country and family, Otto Frank's world began shrinking while Nathan Straus Jr.'s world offered a myriad of possibilities.

After the war Nathan Jr. went back to work at *The Globe* where he was a general editorial assistant. He developed a keen interest in world affairs. By 1920 the U. S. Senate and the American people were grappling with the question, "Would we or would we not join with other nations of the world in establishing a League of Nations to prevent future wars?"[15] Nathan Jr. saw that his own view was contrary to the position of *The Globe*'s conservative Republican leanings. He felt the owner was a good man who stood up for his convictions. But Nathan Jr. didn't agree with the man's politics. He resigned.

He began thinking about public service. His name change in 1910 would certainly give him an advantage; name recognition. After careful consideration, and consulting with local Democratic politicians, Nathan Jr. ran for, and won, a seat in the New York State Legislature in 1920 and was reelected in 1922 and 1924. He said of his terms in office that the work in the State Senate was fascinating and he thoroughly enjoyed it. During this time the Citizens' Union, a non-partisan organization, reported that Nathan Straus Jr. was the member with the best record on votes in either House.

Nathan Straus Jr. - 1917

Nathan Jr. came from a family where many had served in public office. His father was the head of New York City's Department of Health. His uncle Isidor served in the U.S. House of Representatives. And his uncle Oscar was twice Minister to Constantinople, Ambassador to Turkey and Secretary of Commerce and Labor in Theodore Roosevelt's administration. Nathan Jr.'s stint in the legislature deepened his connection to the political arena.

In 1926, with a wife and four small sons to support, Nathan Jr. reluctantly left public life to help his brother Grant and cousin Lee Kohns run the family business, Nathan Straus and Sons, importers of crockery, china and glassware. The firm was once called L. Straus & Sons but the name was changed in 1923, several years after the family split.

Nathan Jr. felt he had to help turn this company into a profitable venture. He bought out his cousin's one-quarter interest in the company and tried to turn the business around with his brother's blessing. Grant was too busy to help because he was concentrating his energies on building the other family business, the Brooklyn, NY department store, Abraham & Straus.

In 1928 the Nathan Straus Jr. family vacationed at Sils-Maria in Switzerland with his college friend Otto Frank and his family. Although we have no corrrespondence between the two men leading up to this date, the familys' vacation shows that the two men stayed in touch and continued their friendship.

Nathan Jr. began to evaluate his business life, how many times he had failed, and how unhappy he was. He wrote that he was contemplating turning his back on business and concentrating on public life. Helen "on various occasions during these years, urged me to do just this ... she noted that I did not seem to be either successful or happy in business."[16]

Nathan Jr. wrote in his unpublished autobiography that eventual success came to Nathan Straus & Sons exactly as it has come in every business in which he succeeded. "I was ignorant of "business" as such, and I did not yet recognize my own greatest weakness, that is, lack of business shrewdness."[17] He later explained that success came when he had the sense of good fortune to enlist as a partner and associate a man who had precisely the qualities that he lacked and still lacked – shrewdness, business acumen, and a knowledge of figures.

When Nathan Sr. died in 1931, Hugh Grant Straus, known as Grant, and Sissie Straus Lehman, Nathan Jr.'s siblings were both successfully involved in their respective lives. Grant successfully ran Abraham & Straus. Sissie was married to Irving Lehman, the Chief Justice of the New York State Appeals Court, the highest court in New York.

Nathan Jr. was in public life and did not have the same economic success as his siblings. To level this inequity, Nathan Sr. left an additional sum in his will to Nathan Jr. as an outright bequest. Rather than deplete the estate's cash, Nathan Jr. took a 24-acre tract of land on the Boston Post Road in the Bronx that had been owned by the family since 1889. In 1934 Nathan Jr. turned it into the country's first housing project, Hillside Homes.

Now the lives of these two friends, Otto and Nathan Jr., began to diverge. Just at a time when conditions in Germany were deteriorating, and Otto Frank's life was taking a downward turn, Nathan Straus Jr. found his calling, affordable housing. The possibilities for him were expanding.

One can also note the powerful friends and allies of Nathan Jr. There were the Lehmans, Fiorello LaGuardia, the mayor of New York City, and the Franklin Delano Roosevelts; people who, under most circumstances, could have solved Otto Frank's problem with a quick phone call.

As a result of his involvement in the Hillside Homes Project, Nathan Jr. became interested in housing progress both in the

United States and abroad. He persuaded New York City's Mayor LaGuardia to appoint him as a special representative of the city to study recent housing developments in England. The report he generated upon his return was well received.

People in the United States knew little about the modern housing techniques as practiced in many countries in Europe. Nathan Jr. believed that, largely as a result of this report, when a vacancy opened up in the New York City Housing Authority in January 1936, he was offered the position. Although he originally refused, Mayor LaGuardia's persistence convinced him to accept. He felt that the experience prepared him for his later role as administrator of the United States Housing Authority.

One must remember that the Great Depression started in 1929 and was still causing difficulties around the world. Otto Frank saw this first hand as his world grew smaller with fewer opportunities for the Jews in Germany. On the other hand, Nathan Jr. was finding his passion, housing. Perhaps it was this very need for low cost housing that created a niche he was able to fill.

During his time in New York City's Housing Authority, Nathan Jr. became politically active. With the support of other housing minded people, and backed by President Roosevelt, Congress came to see housing as a perpetual social obligation. On June 16, 1933, President Roosevelt signed into law the National Industrial Recovery Act (NIRA) under Secretary of the Interior, Harold L. Ickes. Part of the act authorized a comprehensive program of public works including low cost housing and slum clearance.

In 1934 Nathan Jr. became administrator of the National Recovery Administration (NRA) for the state of New York. By November 1937 he was administrator of the United States Housing Authority with a loaning power of $500 million dollars, a position he held until February 1942, two months beyond the disappearance of his friend Otto.

U. S. Secretary of the Interior Harold L. Ickes
and
U. S. Housing Administrator Nathan Straus Jr.
October 20, 1937

Chapter Six – The Straus Family and Immigration

Nathan Jr. came from a philanthropic family. Before World War II and throughout the war's early years, Nathan Straus Jr. was not the only family member who wanted to help family and friends immigrate to the United States. His sister Sissie, who was married to Judge Irving Lehman, also helped many people to immigrate.

There is a family story that Sissie was told by the U. S. State Department during World War II that she could bring no more people to the United States. They said, "No one can have so many relatives." Her cousins Lee and Claire Kohns also sponsored relatives, as did many other members of the family. In some cases, the sponsorship included years of follow up and subsidy until the newcomers were sufficiently established.

Many of the children of these immigrant families spent their summers at a camp set up by Sissie and Irving Lehman on their Portchester, NY property. The children were out of the city for a few weeks, got fresh air, healthy food, sports activities and interaction with other immigrant children. For many, it is the thing they remember most about their early days in the United States.

Nathan Jr. and Helen were also involved in the support of others who wanted their children to be safe during the war. When it appeared that Hitler might conquer England, they invited the son of a business acquaintance to come to New York in 1940. The boy, two year old Niel Sebag-Montefiore and his nanny, lived with the Strauses at their home, Quarry Lake, Westchester County, NY for four years. Niel's family met the Strauses when they were both trying to obtain business assistance for Israel. When it was time for Niel to return to England after the war, he didn't know what his parents looked like and had to be reintroduced to them. Niel and Nathan Jr.'s descendants are still in touch today.

Nathan Jr.'s brother Hugh Grant and his wife Flora Stieglitz Straus also took in an English boy, Edgar Gordon, who lived with them throughout the war. Edgar was the son of one of Lina's relatives. He lived with Nathan and Lina at their Mamaroneck, NY estate during the weekends but lived with other relatives in the city during the week so that he could attend school. He, also, remains in contact with the family after all these years.

There are still people alive today who count their lives as beginning when they arrived in America thanks to the sponsorship of some member of the Straus family. And there were many family members who regretted that they were not able to save more.

Chapter Seven - Case # A-23007
Otto Frank's Dilemma

The blackmail threat by Tonny Ahlers made Otto Frank realize that the Netherlands was no longer a safe place to sit out the war. Although conditions were difficult, and worsening, it seems that Otto Frank still felt that the war could not last forever and that, if he keep a low profile and continued working, his family would be safe - at least until the blackmail threat changed everything. It was early 1941 and it was time to leave.

Rotterdam was bombed by the Germans in May of 1940 reducing most people's ability to escape by sea. In any case, Otto had no way to get to Rotterdam nor did he feel he could move his entire family to the coastal city without a car, which he did not have. The borders were closed and he could think of no other options.

Finally, on April 30, 1941, Otto Frank wrote to his friend Charley, "I am forced to look out for emigration and as far as I can see U.S.A. is the only country we could go to. Perhaps you remember that we have two girls. It is for the sake of the children mainly. ... In 1938 I filed an application at Rotterdam to emigrate to U.S.A. but all the papers have been destroyed there. ... everyone who has an effective affidavit from a member of his family and who can pay his passage may leave. One says that no special difficulties shall be made on the part of the German authorities."[18]

December 11, 1941 was seven months away.

Since Edith Hollander's brothers Julius and Walter were already in America, Otto hoped they could send the necessary affidavits for his family. But they had immigrated only a short time before and Otto was worried that they would not have sufficient capital to make the necessary bank deposits required by the consul. Otto asked his friend for help. "You are the only person I know that

I can ask: Would it be possible for you to give a deposit in my favor?"[19]

When Otto Frank's letter arrived in April 1941, Nathan Straus Jr. was the administrator of the United States Housing Authority in Franklin D. Roosevelt's administration in Washington, DC. Various members of the Straus family had already sponsored many of their relatives and friends, sending the necessary affidavits and making the necessary bank deposits to ensure that they would be allowed to leave Europe. To this day, it is not uncommon to learn of some family member who believes his life, and that of his entire family, was saved because of a Straus' intervention.

In 1941 there was no instant communication, e.mail, Twitter or Blogs. Letters often took more than two weeks to arrive at their overseas destination. Even within the United States, mail took many days.

When requests for assistance were made by perspective émigrés, every suggestion of assistance had to be researched before action could be taken. And then a return letter had to be composed and mailed. Sometimes two or three weeks passed before a response was sent. During that time conditions in Europe continued to deteriorate. Often the situation changed so dramatically that the resolution was voided by a new set of circumstances.

As you read through the following section, notice the dates of the letters being described.

Otto Frank's first letter in this file is dated April 30, 1941. It was mailed to the Straus' New York address. Since Nathan and Helen Straus were living in Washington, D.C. at The Shoreham Hotel, mail was bundled and forwarded on a regular basis to Washington from their New York home. It's possible they didn't receive the letter until three weeks after it was mailed.

After receiving the letter from Otto Frank, Nathan Jr.'s wife, Helen Sachs Straus wrote to Augusta Mayerson, Acting Director of the Migration Department of the National Refugee Service on May 28,1941. It was almost a month between the time Otto Frank wrote his letter and Helen Straus acted upon it. Certainly if Nathan Jr. and Helen had received Otto's April letter in a timely manner, they would have acted much more quickly.

Helen wrote, "After all the letters - requests for help we've had from people we hardly know, the enclosed one from Mr. Frank, - from my husband's best friend during their university years - an extraordinarily fine man - as you can tell from the letter."[20] She asked what could be done to help the Frank family.

December 11th was now six months away.

On June 3rd, Augusta Mayerson wrote to Nathan Straus in Washington, D.C. suggesting that: 1. Nathan write directly to Otto Frank reassuring him of his interest and telling Otto that he is preparing the necessary affidavits of support. A covering letter would be sent to the American consul in Amsterdam explaining the reason for the Strauses interest in the Frank family's immigration and concern for their welfare. In this letter Miss Mayerson also suggested that Nathan write that he hoped the affidavit and accompanying documents would satisfy the American consul so that the customary deposit of $5,000 would not be necessary. 2. Miss Mayerson told Nathan she would write to Otto Frank's brothers-in-law telling them of Nathan's support and his intention to send affidavits but that, since the Strauses were not related to the Frank family, that it would be advisable for the Hollander brothers to also send affidavits of support "to strengthen the applicant's chance for a visa." 3. Miss Mayerson continued to advise that her agency would cable the overseas committee "requesting information and instructions in the matter of steamship reservations." She thought that Otto Frank might be able to turn over sufficient funds to the relief agency for special consideration for the purchase of the tickets.

will be able in your year to the will of spend enough efficient
funds to give him special consideration for the purchase of tickets

June 3rd
1 9 4 1

AIRMAIL

Mr. Nathan Straus
The Shoreham
Connecticut Avenue at Calvert Street
Washington, D. C.

In reply please refer to:
FRANK, Otto
Merwedelaan 37
Amsterdam, Holland
Case # A-23057

My dear Mr. Straus:

Mrs. Straus and I discussed over the telephone the contents of the
letter which you received from Mr. Otto Frank and agreed to suggest
the following procedure:

1. That you will undoubtedly wish to write directly to Mr. Frank
in answer to his letter, in which you may wish to reassure him of
your interest and advise him that you are preparing affidavits of
support on behalf of him and his family. That your affidavits
will be accompanied by a covering letter from you to the American
consul in Amsterdam stating the reasons for your interest in
Mr. Frank and his family and your concern about their welfare.
That you hope your affidavit and the accompanying documents will
satisfy the American consul, so that no deposit of $5000 will be
necessary.

2. I will write to the brothers-in-law at your suggestion telling
them of your interest and that you are preparing an affidavit of
support for the American consul in Amsterdam. I will suggest to
the brothers-in-law, that since you are not related to Mr. Frank,
it is most desirable that one or both of them also send affidavits
of support to strengthen the applicant's chance for visas.

3. With regard to overseas transportation, we will be pleased to
cable the committee abroad requesting information and instructions
in the matter of steamship reservations. It may be that Mr. Frank
will be able to turn over to the relief agency abroad sufficient
funds to give him special consideration for the purchase of tickets

70

-2-

Mr. Nathan Straus   June 3rd, 1941
Washington, D. C.

through the committee abroad. We will send this cable
after your affidavits have been forwarded to the American
consul in Amsterdam.

For your convenience, we are enclosing five affidavit of
support forms.

With kind regards,

                                        Very sincerely yours,

                                        Augusta Mayerson
                                        Acting Director
                                        Migration Department

enc.
AM:mr

On June 3rd, Miss Mayerson wrote to Miss Susan Kramer of the National Refugee Service, Inc. asking if Miss Kramer would contact the authorities in Massachusetts to learn about Walter and Julius Hollander's situation and their ability to help.

At that time one needed an affidavit from a United States citizen willing to be a sponsor. Otto Frank also needed a trust fund placed in his name. Recognizing that a relative would have more influence than a family friend, Nathan Jr. suggested that Edith Frank's two brothers, Julius and Walter Hollander, who were living in Massachusetts, would be better sponsors for the Franks. The Boston Committee for Refugees, an agency founded in 1935 to aid European immigrants, was contacted with all the information.

On June 9th Miss Mayerson wrote to Mr. Maurice Krinsky of the Boston Committee for Refugees explaining the information in the previous letters and asking for further information. "We feel, nevertheless, that since the Franks are not related to the Strauses, it is advisable that the brothers-in-law submit documents as well since the American Consul always looks with greater favor upon documents submitted by relatives … An affidavit from a relative always strengthens an applicant's chances for a visa. We shall appreciate if you would discuss with Mr. Hollander … the matter of transportation for this family since that is extremely important in view of the fact that the American Consul abroad are not issuing any visa unless a specific booking is available to the prospective immigrant."[21]

In addition to all the affidavits, the Franks would have to prove they had their ship's ticket before they could get their visas issued.

The Boston Committee for Refugees located both Hollander brothers, investigated their living conditions, income and business prospects. It was found that both brothers had recently immigrated and did not have sufficient income to support the

Frank family. To counter that, Nathan Jr. offered to put up the necessary money. The committee was concerned that the Frank family was too large for one sponsor.

The need to dot the i's and cross the t's was costing valuable time.

Julius and Walter agreed to sponsor their mother, Rosa Hollander, who was living with the Franks. On June 11th Nathan Jr. sent a letter of sponsorship for Otto and Edith Frank. Anne and Margot were sponsored by the Hollander brothers' employers. Now the entire family had sponsorship.

To speed the process, Nathan Jr. turned to the National Refugee Service. It was their role to cut through the many layers of red tape within the U. S. government and to sort through all of the requirements to get the Frank family to America.

Since Nathan Jr. was in FDR's administration, and since his family had been politically active in the U. S. for a very long time, it is reasonable to expect that he, if anyone, would be able to cut through the red tape and bureaucratic requirements. At least that seemed like a reasonable expectation.

Less than a month had passed since Otto Frank's letter was forwarded to Augusta Mayerson of the National Refugee Service who set the wheels in motion. The Hollander brothers were located. Sponsors were found. All the sponsors and their affidavits were ready. Everyone agreed to help and do everything within their power to bring the Frank family to America.

But everyone underestimated the malevolence of red tape. On June 16th Miss Mayerson wrote to the Strauses about a new regulation that would go into effect after July 1st. All documents would have to go to the Department of State in Washington DC for review before being sent to Europe. She suggested that it was likely a new form of affidavit would be required. Since the Frank's documents were prepared and ready to leave, Miss Mayerson thought the papers that were ready should be retained in the U. S. until the new regulations were enacted.

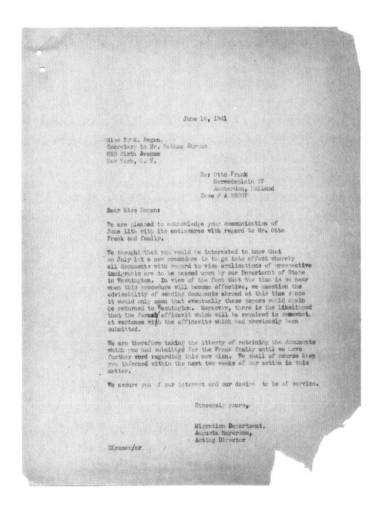

Here was a situation where each person and each agency involved agreed to do what was necessary to bring the Frank family to America. All of the necessary paperwork was completed. But a change in a form caused a two-week delay in the papers being sent back to Europe. Those two weeks proved disastrous.

One June 28th Augusta Mayerson wrote to Nathan Straus Jr. describing the current situation with regard to the Frank family's immigration status. "We were advised that a Mr. Julius Hollander and his brother Walter had provided affidavits for Mr. and Mrs. Frank and their family. Another affidavit had been given for the mother of the two brothers Hollander. These were sent to Holland on May 10, 1941. Mr. Walter Hollander procured a supplementary affidavit of support from his employer, another affidavit was given by another stranger. The latter two affidavits were used for the two children of Mr. Otto Frank. The affidavit submitted by Julius and Walter Hollander were for Mr. and Mrs. Frank and for their mother, Mrs. Rosa Hollander, who is living with the Franks in Holland."[22]

Amazingly, Julius and Walter's employers submitted affidavits of support for Margot and Anne. Each man had only known one Hollander brother for a short time and neither knew anyone else in the Frank family. It was a huge personal commitment.

Now the entire Frank family had affidavits. The employers of Julius and Walter Hollander would send the affidavits for Anne and Margot. Edith Frank's brother, Julius and Walter Hollander would send affidavits for their mother, Rosa. And Nathan Straus Jr. would send the necessary affidavits for Edith and Otto Frank.

Miss Mayerson continued in her June 28th letter, "We were advised that Julius Hollander is employed as a night oven man by the Canton Japanning Company of Canton, Mass. He averages $28.00 a week. He is unmarried. Mr. Walter Hollander is also unmarried. He averages $20.00 a week. The two brothers have a joint account totaling $2,900. $1,200 of this sum actually belongs to Mrs. Rosa Hollander, the mother. We learned that transportation has not as yet been arranged for the Franks and Mrs. Rosa Hollander.

"When interviewed, Julius and Walter Hollander wondered whether some help might be given to their relatives toward their transportation. They stated that the money which they were holding would have to be used for the maintenance of this family group after their arrival in the United States. The brothers indicated that they would assume responsibility for the prospective immigrants after their arrival.

"We are informed that Mr. Otto Frank had previously visited the United States and had worked at one time at Macy's. According to the relatives, he has a thorough command of the English language.

"In view of the recent Executive Orders which came through with reference to visa applicants we did not feel that there was any point in forwarding the affidavits that you kindly executed in behalf of this family. As you know a new type of affidavit will now have to be prepared after July 1, 1941. Moreover, affidavits will now be evaluated in the Visa Division of the State Department who will pass upon the adequacy of these. It is only after the State Department reaches a decision that the American Consul abroad is notified of such approval and may then issue a visa to the applicant, providing they meet all other requirements such as physical examination and so forth. The American Consul will retain the privilege of denying a visa to the applicant if in his opinion the applicant fails to meet these other requirements. It is also important to ascertain whether the Franks and Mrs. Hollander have any close relations in Germany and German occupied territories of Italy whom they would leave behind, since visas might be denied them.

"We realize that with the Consulate offices closing in Germany and German occupied territory the Franks and Mrs. Hollander may have some difficulty in applying for visas, but we are hopeful that the German authorities will permit refugees who are ready to leave the country, to go to a place where a Consulate office is functioning."[23]

Everything was in place. The Hollander brothers were willing to do anything within their power to help their family immigrate. Their employers were willing to sponsor Anne and Margot. The Strauses were willing to put up the money for the Frank's transportation and the United States was willing to take them in.

What went wrong?
Timing!

The Franks were German, not Dutch, and this added a serious complication. The American Consulate in Netherlands was closed and they had nowhere to go for the required visa.

On June 30th Otto wrote to Charley, "I received your kind letter of June 14th and have to thank you again and again for all you are doing. You already did more than I thought could be done. I know that you are not a friend of long talks, but you certainly know quite well how I feel about it. It is a pity that for the present all efforts will be useless as the AMERICAN CONSULATE at ROTTERDAM is leaving and nobody knows as yet if things will be handled further or not. So we have to wait. Bad luck, but cannot be helped. Let us hope that conditions will get more normal again. As soon as I hear that there are chances still I shall let you know and you certainly will be informed still better than I am about the possibilities which remain."[24]

The American Consulate General suspended action on these visas on June 30th. On July 1st Nathan Jr. wrote to Otto Frank, "I have taken up the matter of your immigration to this country with the National Refugee Service. I have also discussed it with the State Department officials as I would very much like to help you. I am afraid the news is not good news. Unless you can get to a place where there is an American Consul, there does not seem to be any way of arranging for you to come over. I am informed that there are still American Consuls in Portugal, Spain, Free France and Switzerland. These are the only countries in which a visa can be arranged."[25]

June 30 th 1941

Dear Charley,

I received your kind letter of June 4th and have
to thank you again and again for all your are
doing. Your already did more than I thought could
be done. I know that you are not a friend of long
talks, but you certainly know quite well how I
feel about it.

It is a pity that for the present all efforts
will be useless as the AMERICAN CONSULATE at
ROTTERDAM is leaving and nobody knows as yet if
things will be handled further or not. So we have
to wait. Bad luck, but cannot be helped. Let us
hope that conditions will get more normal again.
As soon as I hear that there are chances still
I shall let you know and you certainly will be
informed still better than I am about the possibilities which remain.

In the meantime all the best to you all and
kindest regards from Edith and myself.

Cordially yours

People were not being issued visas unless they could show that
they already had tickets on a ship to the U. S. Because of this new
requirement, new visa applications had to be made and each new
application form was sent to Washington D.C. for screening.

By mid July 1941 the German consulates in America were ordered closed. Germany retaliated by closing all American consulates in their country and in all of their occupied territories.

Otto Frank and his family would now have to reach a consulate in a neutral country before being able to leave for America. Spain and Portugal had the closest open consulate. But the Franks needed exit visas to leave their country of domicile too. And the Franks couldn't obtain exit visias. They were unable to travel without exit visas from the Netherlands and transit visas to go through the countries on their route to Portugal.

Now there were only four months remaining until December 11th.

Augusta Mayerson wrote to Maurice Krinsky of the Boston Committee for Refugees on August 13th. "We thought you would be interested to know that Mr. Nathan Straus wrote directly to Mr. Otto Frank, informing him that he had discussed the immigration problem of his family with the State Department officials and that he had been advised that unless the Franks will be able to go to a country in which there is an American Consular service available, no affidavits will be accepted in their behalf, by Washington.

"Mr. Straus indicated that at any time when the Frank family will be able to proceed to a neutral country, he will then be glad to help them."[26]

December 11th was three months away when Nathan Jr. wrote to Otto on September 11th, "I am prepared to submit the necessary affidavits of support just as soon as you are able to assure me that you can leave Holland and get permission to go to a country where there is an American Consul."[27]

Nathan Jr. suggested that his friend call on the Joodische Raad Voor Amsterdam, the Jewish Council for Amsterdam, for possible assistance. Under the new American visa regulations, Otto did not qualify for an American visa because he had relatives remaining in German territories. And, in addition, aliens from Germany were considered undesirable, even those who were trying to flee because of the German policies toward the Jews. Otto Frank and his family were concerned that they would not be able to obtain the necessary visas despite the assistance of Nathan Straus Jr., Edith's brothers Julius and Walter Hollander and the cooperation of several agencies in America.

Back in the United States, Nathan, Jr. worked diligently to accumulate the information necessary to sponsor Otto Frank and his family. Otto had already concluded that they would not be permitted to go to the United States directly. He began looking for alternate routes for immigration.

At the time Cuba was allowing people to enter on tourist visas. On September 8, 1941, crossing Nathan's letter of September 11th, Otto wrote to Nathan, "The only way to get to a neutral country are visas of other states such as Cuba ... and many of my acquaintances got visas for Cuba."[28]

The fee was steep; $250 per person in direct payment and $2,500 per person for the visa and bonds. The $2,500 was to be refunded when the person left Cuba. In 2102 dollars, $4,000 is $40,000.

The letters in the newly discovered Otto Frank file show that Nathan Straus, Jr., Julius and Walter Hollander and the National Refugee Service were investigating this option.

On September 17th Julius Hollander wrote to Nathan, Jr., "I have information that transit visas for Cuba are available again. I would appreciate it if you would assist me in obtaining a visa for Mr. Otto Frank as soon as possible. My brother and I will share expenses with you. ... It would be impossible for us to obtain an immigration visa for this country without your assistance. My brother and I will pay for all of Mr. Frank's expenses while he is in Cuba."[29]

Augusta Mayerson sent a telegram from the National Refugee Service in New York on September 19, 1941 to the Joodsche

80

Raad Voor in Amsterdam. It read, "can otto frank merwedeplein thirtyseven secure exit permit transit visa Spain friend preparing affidavits cable reply."[30]

Miss Mayerson wrote to Nathan Straus Jr. on October 2nd to let him know that there had been no response to the cable she'd sent. She told Nathan Jr. she'd learned that "Germany is not issuing exit permits to persons between the ages of eighteen and forty-five, who are at present residing in Germany or German-occupied areas. Our correspondence does not reveal the exact ages of Otto and Edith Frank.

"In view of the fact that chances for emigration to the United States for persons in occupied areas are so poor, Mr. Hollander presents through his letter to you an alternative plan, - this is the emigration of the Frank family to Cuba.

"Only two types of visas are available to refugees – tourist and transit visas. A tourist visa may be obtained if the following conditions are met: A $2,000 deposit in the Bank of Cuba to cover maintenance for the applicant, who may draw upon it immediately upon his arrival in Cuba; a $500 bond posted with the Cuban government to ensure against the applicant's becoming a public charge; a $150 deposit with the steamship company to cover outgoing passage from Cuba.

"A transit visa may be obtained if the applicant holds a valid visa for another country. In that case, only a $500 bond is deposited, and $150 for outgoing passage is necessary. The cost in meeting legal fees and visa charges comes to approximately $250 per person. ...

"Because of the fluctuating administrative rulings in the Cuban government, the National Refugee service does not take responsibility for negotiating for these visas. ... There are always risks involved where Cuba is concerned."[31]

Perhaps Ms. Mayerson was referring to the ill-fated journey of the SS. St. Louis, a ship of mostly German Jewish refugees that arrived in Cuba in May 1939. Cuban president Frederico Laredo Bru tightened immigration restrictions and refused to let the refugees disembark when they arrived even though each possessed a tourist visa for Cuba. These refugees were taken to South America where each country also refused them entry. They even sailed up the southeastern coast of the United States before being turned away. The United States had already filled its German quota and the administration was afraid to risk the anger of Congress by taking in more refugees.

The St. Louis returned to Europe where Great Britain, France, Belgium and Netherlands each took a portion of the passengers. 288 people were admitted to Great Britain. All but one survived the war. Netherlands took 181, France took 224 and Belgium took the remaining 214 passengers of the St. Louis. Of the 619 passengers who returned to Western Europe, 187 emigrated before Germany invaded Western Europe in May 1940. 532 St. Louis passengers were trapped after the German invasion. Only 278 survived the Holocaust.[32]

On October 6th Julius Hollander wrote, "Referring to your last letter, I suggest that you get in touch with the German-Jewish Children Aid, Inc. in regards to bringing over the Frank children from Amsterdam.

"My brother and I will pay for the boat ticket and Cuban visas for Mr. Frank. If you give the necessary deposit to the Cuban Government for Mr. Frank, I promise you that it will be returned to you untouched..."[33]

Now only two months remained until December 11th. One can feel the growing desperation in each suceeding letter as everyone who was involved tried to find a way to bring the Frank family to the U.S.

Letters and cables continued to be sent between the National Refugee Service, the Boston Committee for Refugees, Joodsche Raad Voor Amsterdam (Jewish Council for Amsterdam), Nathan Straus, Jr., Julius Hollander and Otto Frank. In each case there was agreement. Everyone wanted to help the Frank family reach America. But nothing could be done to expedite their immigration. The ever changing red tape became a colossal obstacle.

On October 12th the Joodsche Raad Voor Amsterdam finally wrote to the National Refugee Service, "As Mr. Straus has written himself that the State Department will accept his affidavit, Mr. Otto Frank is of the opinion that he perhaps need not at all go to Cuba, so that the money deposited for the irrevocable credit as well as for the landing deposit, may be returned unused after Mr. Frank and his family have received their U.S.A. visas to be secured by Mr. Nathan Straus and the members of the Frank-Hollander family."[34]

Otto wrote to Nathan Jr. on October 12th. One can see the difficulties in communication from Otto's opening paragraph. "I had a letter from the Joodsche raad giving me notice about a telegram received re. exitpermit and transitvisa Spain. As the Joodsche raad does not send the telegrams himself they did not sent me to the firm Hoyman & Schuurman, who have permission to send cables about visas. They answered but their telegram was sent to the Joint (Joint Distribution Committee) instead of the Nat. Refugee Serv. and as the Joint cabled that they did not know about the matter, I had the answer addressed to you. Afterwards the joodsche raad told me, that it was not the Joint who had cabled but the National Refugee Service and the fault had been corrected."[35]

Imagine the amount of time wasted while all of this was being straightened out!

Otto's October 12th letter continued, "Only after having received a cable of this sort one can apply for the permit to leave Holland

and after having received this one gets the Transitvisum Spain. It is all much more difficult as one can imagine and is getting more complicated every day."[36]

Augusta Mayerson wrote to Julius Hollander on October 17th, "We are informed by the German Jewish Childrens Aid Incorporated, that it is almost impossible for them to bring out children at this time from Amsterdam. ... In view of the ultimate plan which is, as we understand it, to bring the family to the United States, there is a real question as to the wisdom of helping Mr. Frank to immigrate to Cuba alone. The fact that his wife and children remain in occupied area abroad would militate against his application for the United States visa from Cuba."[37]

On October 17th Augusta Mayerson wrote to Maurice Krinsky of the Boston Committee for Refugees who was acting as the liaison between the various parties and the Hollander brothers. Her letter expressed Nathan Jr.'s concern that the large sum of money necessary to help the Frank family get to Cuba was not refundable and that, if they could not obtain the visas, this sum would be forfeited. She wrote, "Mr. and Mrs. Nathan Straus are very much interested in helping Otto Frank and his family, but this is only one of many cases that the Strauses are interested in and they are not prepared to invest the large sum of money that is indicated in the matter of Cuban visas for the family. They think it is highly desirable to keep the family together. Even after all this money had been deposited and invested there is still the question as to whether the family could succeed in obtaining the necessary exit permits and transit visas. We believe that Mr. and Mrs. Straus would be willing it participate financially in bringing the family out of Cuba, provided the Hollanders in Massachusetts are able to carry a good part of the financial burden."[38]

Julius Hollander responded though Maurice Krinsky on October 21st, "... he and his brother are prepared to pay $1500 toward the immigration of the Franks. Mr. Hollander said that Mr. Strauss [sic] can use these funds in whatever way he wishes to assist the

Franks."[39] This amount is $24,000 in 2012 dollars, an enormous amount by anyone's measure.

Krinsky's letter stated, "Mr. Hollander assured us that once the family arrived in Cuba, he would be willing to render all the support necessary to enhance their welfare and there would be no further demand made upon Mr. Strauss [sic]."[40]

On October 27th Krinsky added, "He and his brother have asked us to inform you that they will "repay every amount given for the immigration of relatives and we will begin to pay these sums immediately each month."[41] We can almost feel the Hollander brother's desparation. They would do anything to help their relatives get out of war torn Europe.

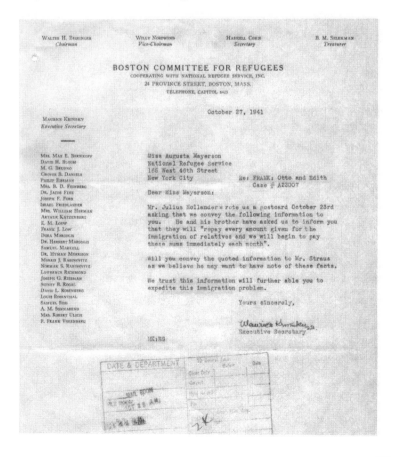

Critical weeks were lost as people maneuvered to avoid losing money. In all fairness, America was not at war and the "Final Solution" was not yet promulgated. Hindsight must be suspended.

At the end of October Cecilia Razovsky of the National Refugee Service wrote to Augusta Mayerson expressing her doubt that U.S. visas would be issued for children whose parents were still in occupied territories.

There were less than six weeks remaining until December 11th.

Letters throughout November worked out the details of how Otto Frank could obtain the Cuban visas. The Strauses agreed to arrange the bond and pay for transportation costs. The Hollander brothers would pay the attorney fees, visa fees and outgoing passage fees from Cuba.

Augusta Mayerson wrote to Helen Straus on November 12th: "The enclosed copy of a letter from our Committee in Amsterdam speaks for itself. Please note that they are including the mother-in-law, Rosa Hollander. The Committee's reference to Mr. Frank's "opinion that he perhaps need not at all go to Cuba" probably means that when he gets to the neutral country, Spain or Portugal, he hopes to be able to obtain United States visas. I am afraid that he is rather optimistic and I am writing back to the Amsterdam Committee explaining the situation more fully."[42]

Ms. Mayerson wrote to Julius Hollander on November 12th, "It takes from ten to twenty-one days to obtain a legal Cuban visa. We have recently been informed that persons in occupied areas are being denied exit permits. It may be that even after the Franks have obtained Cuban visas they may fail to obtain the necessary exit permits from Holland."[43]

On November 18th Julius Hollander wrote to the Strauses, "The National Refugee Service, Inc. informed me on November 12 of your decision to contribute in a generous way to the immigration of Mr. Otto Frank and family. ... The most important issue for the time being is the providing of the exit permits. Because I was advised not to pay for the Cuban Visa before I would be informed by my brother-in-law that exit permits would be granted, I sent a cable to Amsterdam asking him to make sure that the permits are available."[44]

Julius then wrote to the National Refugee Service on the 22nd, "Whereupon I cabled again to make positively sure, that exit permits would be given, before I would be able to deposit amount for visas and tickets."[45]

Otto Frank's travel agent in Amsterdam cabled, "Exit permit can only be given after Cuban visa is sent over. Please care only for Otto Frank for the time being to confine financial risk."[46]

Augusta Mayerson cabled Julius Hollander on the 27th, "If you and brother start negotiations for Cuban visas ... Mrs. Straus willing make necessary deposits ... for Otto Edith Margot Anne Frank. Its up to you to start if interested."[47] Julius Hollander responded, "This morning I got a cable from Amsterdam in which Mr. Otto Frank is asking for one visa only because he wants to find out if exit permits are still available. In case they are not available, only $275 will be lost."[48]

On the 28th of November Julius Hollander ordered the Cuban exit permit. He wrote to Augusta Mayerson, " ... I instructed the Compass Travel Bureau to take out the Cuban Visa for Mr Otto Frank. I told them to communicate with you ... Please assure the Compass to expedit [sic] the transaction because, if Mr Frank can get the exit permit, the rest of the family will follow and we will give them the business."[49]

An interoffice memo to Augusta Mayerson dated December 11, 1941 stated, "Mr. Hollander of Compass Bureau called to say that the application for Cuban visas for Otto Frank has been cancelled."[50]

Dear Mrs Mayer-John   Canton November 28, 41

Kindly referring to my letter of yesterday I instructed the Compass Travel Bureau to take out the Cuban Visa for Mr Otto Frank. I told them to communicate with you and that I would put up the 275 Dollars. Please assure the Compass to expedite the transaction because, if Mr Frank can get the escape permit, the rest of the family will follow and we will give them the business. Yours very sincerely J. Hollander

Most of 1941 was squandered doing the right thing in the right way. Otto Frank was still trying everything possible to help his family. He thought he could get to Cuba and then send for his wife, children and mother-in-law.

Although Otto Frank's single visa was finally issued on December 1st, no one knows if it ever reached him.

Inevitably, December 11, 1941 arrived. Germany and Italy declared war on the United States. Cuba cancelled its visa program. And the Frank's disappeared.

Conditions around the world were deteriorating. The doors to immigration were closing or already closed. Americans began to fear that anyone with family left behind would be coerced into acting as a spy or saboteur. Xenophobia, the fear or hatred of aliens of foreigners, or anything strange and unfamiliar, was rampant in the United States at this time.

Professor Breitman wrote about 1941-1942 "According to the State Department legal advisor, the Supreme Court had repeatedly emphasized that aliens had no right of entry, and, "at times like this, when the safety of the country is imperiled, it seems fully justified to resolve any possible doubts in favor of the country, rather than in favor of the aliens concerned."[51]

FDR had established the War Refugee Board to act as the liaison between those wanting to get out of Europe and those wanting to help them immigrate. We can see by the examples of this one case study that Augusta Mayerson worked very hard to help the Frank family. And we can see how she worked with the other agencies, the Hollander brothers and Nathan Straus Jr. toward the same goal.

David S. Wyman stated in his book, *Paper Walls: America and the Refugee Crisis 1938-1941* "The War Refugee Board, which FDR established to save Jews and other victims of the Nazis, had little power, almost no cooperation from FDR, his administrators and was grossly underfunded."[52]

After the Great Depression, Americans worried that the new immigrants would take their jobs. Between 1929 and 1941 the feeling of many Americans turned nationalistic. America for Americans was often heard.

A month after Germany declared war on the United States, Jews in Amsterdam were being sent to Nazi work camps. The Frank family continued to live quietly, trying to avoid the attention of the Germans or the Dutch Nazis in their midst. Although conditions for the Jewish immigrants in Netherlands continued to deteriorate, it is possible to believe, based on what we know about the man, that Otto Frank must have presented his family with a positive outlook and reassurance that the unpleasantness would soon pass.

Six months after the end of the correspondence between Otto Frank and Nathan Straus Jr., the Frank family went into hiding in the attic of Prinsengracht 263. Communication between the two families was cut off at the end of November 1941.

The story of what happened to the Frank family from this point on is well known and will not be retold here.

It is only through the newly discovered correspondence between Otto Frank and Nathan Straus Jr. that we can begin to understand Otto Frank's personality, the political climate he and his family were faced with and how that evolved, how hard he tried to leave Europe and how many others tried to help. The recently discovered letters clearly add a new dimension to this family's tragic experience.

Chapter Eight: After the War

After the end of the European war, on June 22, 1945, a letter by G. V. Saxl of the Migration Department describes Julius Hollander's efforts to contact his family. He had been advised that they were in Paris. Apparently he didn't know at that time that only Otto Frank survived. He was anxious to begin the immigration process on behalf of his sister Edith and her family.

On June 26, 1945 a letter by Ann S. Petluck, director of the Migration Service states, "We have been advised that the above mentioned family reached France recently."[53]

Letters from various agencies report that efforts to reach the Frank family were unsuccessful.

Otto Frank wrote to his college friend for the first time after the war on September 24, 1945. Nathan Jr. was the president of WMCA radio, a New York based radio station. "Dear Charley, you told me once that I am the only one who calls you by this name, but I feel more like the old relations between us if I still call you by that name."[54]

He said that he didn't want to write until he'd learned if Nathan's four sons were safe. Each of the four Straus boys served their country during the war. "I don't know if you ever received my last letters in 1941 thanking you for all you did. It was a great support for us all even if we had no success. You cannot know how glad we all were and how we appreciated your friendship. Too late. Now you probably know the fate of my dear wife and my girls. I don't want to write about them in detail it cannot help any more. I have to bear my fate.

"I suppose you have heard and read about the horrors of the Polish Concentration Camps. It surpasses all imagination. Luckily I lived there only for a few months, but even then every hour one is under the caprice of those tormentors is too much. Luckily, I was in the hospital for some time and that I was rescued.

"Now I am back again and try to start a new life. I lost all I ever had, all our household having been looted by the Germans. But all that does not much trouble me. I am not in need, as I get from my old firm what I need. ... Being alone, at your age, my personal life does not interest me very much. It is for others that I try to do my best."[55]

Nathan Straus, Jr. wrote to Otto at Prinsengracht 263 in Amsterdam the next day, "Both Helen and I were glad to receive your letter and thus have direct personal news of you. Of course, ... we have heard indirectly of the tragic events that have befallen your family. Words are quite useless in such a situation as this. In fact, the huge scale of the tragedy which has befallen innocent people is almost beyond the human mind to encompass.

"As for ourselves, it will interest you to know that we hope shortly all four boys will be out of uniform and back in civilian life."[56]

Otto's response is dated November 14, 1945. "I am delighted having received your kind letter of Oct. 25 and to get personal news from you and Helen. It always does good if one feels that there are old friends who still care for you. I must not complain.

"In the meantime the bank called up and handed me the amount you spoke of. Well, I do not know how to thank you even if you wrote; forget it! I know you don't like me to speak about it but nevertheless I thank you with all my heart. Even if I am not really in need, I don't own much and the amount will help me and others along, as I always use part of what I earn for others, especially orphans at the moment, who want to join their families abroad or to go to Palestine. Apart from business I am very busy copying the diary of my youngest daughter (which was found by chance) and to find an editor for it. I am going to let you know more about it later.

"I dont give up and try to build up again. Let us hope that it will be possible to meet again one day. I never forget you and I never forget your parents."[57]

Mr. Nathan Straus
YMCA inc.
1657 Broadway
New York   Nov. 14 th 1945

Dear Charley,
I am delighted having received your kind letter of Oct. 25
and to get personal news from you and Hlen. It always does
good if one feels that there are old friends who still care
for you! I must not complain.
In the mean time the bank called up and handed me the amount
you soke of. Well, I do not know how to thank you even if
you wrote; forget it! I know you dont like me to speak about
it but nevertheless I thank you with all my hearty
Even if I am not really in need I dont own much and the amount
will help me and others along, as I always use part of what
I earn for others, especially orphans at the moment, who
want to join there families abroad or to go to Palestine.
Apart from business I am very busy in copying the diary of
my yongest daughter (which was found by chance) and to
find a editor for it. I am going to let you know more about
it later.
I received a clipping giving me details about the marriage
of your son and I wish you, Helen and the jong couple all
the best.
From Lili I had a very nice letter. She always was a darling.
My mother is going to be 80 in December and I hope to be able
to go to Switzerland to see her. Being "staatenlos" everything
is doubbel difficult!
I dont give up and try to build up again. Let us hope that
it will possible to meet again one day. I never forget you
and I never forgot your parents.
Believe me to be, ever
                                    Yours

By January 31, 1946 Ms. Petluck director of the Migration Service wrote, "... we are in receipt of a report advising us that Otto Frank is reputed to be living at 263 Prinsengracht, Amsterdam. They mentioned that Mrs. Edith Hollander is deceased and that the daughters are still missing."[58]

Julius Hollander wrote to an unknown recipient on February 2, 1946, "Thank you for the good letter of January 31 and the interest you have shown, but I am in contact with Otto Frank and he wants to stay in Amsterdam."[59]

Feb 2, 1946

Gentlemen

I thank you for your letter of January 31 and the interest you have shown, but I am in contact with Otto Frank and he wants to stay in Amsterdam.

Very sincerely yours

Julius Hollander

Re Frank otto & family
Case A23007

Ann S. Petluck responded that they made note of Otto Frank's desire to remain in Amsterdam and that her agency, the Migration Department, would cooperate if he changed his mind at a later date.

After the war people tried to find out what happened to their relatives. Many agencies had forms that could be filled out and left with them. When information became available, it would be relayed to the relatives.

94

A National Refugee Service application for location was filled out by Emma Stern Darmstadt, Otto Frank's second cousin. She was asking about the Frank family. The form states that Edith Frank died of starvation, that Anne and Margot were deported for slave labor, and that Otto Frank was deported to Poland where he almost died of starvation. He was freed by the Russians when they liberated Auschwitz, taken to Odessa and sailed back to Amsterdam. Edith and Otto were at Auschwitz Concentration Camp. Anne and Margot were shipped to Auschwitz and then transferred to Bergen-Belsen where they died of typhus within days of each other shortly before the end of the war.

After returning to Amsterdam and reconnecting with his former employees who were keeping Opekta running, Miep Gies gave Otto the pages of Anne's diary. They were found in the attic after the family was taken away. Otto wanted to keep the diary private but was convinced by several friends that he had an obligation to Anne to have the manuscript published. He worked with several translators and editors until he was satisfied. Many thought it was too soon after the war. People were trying to forget the atrocities and there was doubt about interest in the musings of a Jewish teenage girl. The book was rejected by five British publishing houses and nine in the US.

Anne's diary was first published in book form in Holland in 1947 under the title, *Het Achterhuis*, (*The Out House*). After several unsuccessful releases and more editing the diary was rereleased by Doubleday in the United States in 1952 under the title *Anne Frank: The Diary of a Young Girl*. A preface was written by Eleanor Roosevelt at the urging of her friend Nathan Straus Jr. It quickly became one of the world's bestselling books.

By the time of Otto's death in 1980, more than 14 million copies had been sold in 50 languages. Today it has been translated into 67 languages and more than 75 million copies have been sold. Schools around the world require their students to read the diary.

When the 1952 English language version of *Anne Frank: The Diary of a Young Girl*, was released, Nathan Jr wrote to Otto Frank, "I cannot tell you how touched I was at receiving the copy of your daughter's book. You can be certain that Helen and I will read it immediately with real understanding and appreciation. It must be a satisfaction to you to be able to render this belated and insufficient tribute to your daughter.

"The fact that Mrs. Roosevelt has written the introduction will mean more than you can imagine to American readers. Helen and I have been personal friends of hers for a great many years, but there are millions in this country who feel they know her as a friend, because of her unmatched record of devotion to the public service, her writings, her contacts with people of all kinds all over the world, and, of course, her daily articles or column published in scores of American newspapers."[60]

Helen Straus wrote on July 7th, "All of us who read the book – and there will be many indeed, will always have a deeper insight into an adolescent girl's problems and certainly a greater awareness of what those war years meant in terms of family hardship.

"You must be very, very proud that Anne could do this for the world, even though she died before she had the chance to fulfill the promise of the talent that was hers."[61]

Otto responded to Helen's letter, "It was so charming of you to write me about Anne's book and I must tell you that all you write is giving me consolation and faith. I regard this work on the book as a mission and want it published in many countries in order to help people to understand each other and to build a better world."[62]

Doubleday, the publisher of Anne's book, urged Otto Frank to allow the book to be adapted for the theater, radio and for television. Otto asked Nathan to advise him as he had little experience or knowledge in this area. He planned to come to New York on a visitor's visa. Nathan and Helen invited him to stay with them at the New York City apartment and at their country home, Quarry Lake, in Westchester County, NY home.

In January Nathan wrote, "The theme of Anne's diary seems to me a universal one. The fact that it was written by a Jewish girl is a very fine thing for any Jew. But, so far as the world is concerned, it would seem to me a distinct advantage if the play were written by a non-Jew. In the first place, that would emphasize the universality of the theme. In the second place, there is, to my mind, little doubt but that the play would be much more readily accepted on its merits if it were written by a non-Jew." Helen added, "I think that Ann's diary is much bigger than just a 'Jewish story.'"[63]

Meyer Levin, who read the diary in French in 1950, drafted a play from the manuscript. Levin was an American correspondent during the war and saw firsthand the destruction of human life in the concentration camps. He was deeply moved by this experience. He wrote to Otto Frank asking for the rights to the book and subsequent play and movie to be made from it. Otto had already committed to the publication of the diary by Doubleday but Levin wrote a screenplay.

Otto wrote to Nathan Jr. during the negotiations about the script asking for advice. Unfortunately a series of misunderstandings led to Levin suing the producers of the play and also Otto Frank. Otto asked Nathan to find him a good lawyer. Former director of YIVO, Carl J. Rheins, wrote, "... it was Nathan Straus III who introduced Otto in 1952 to his attorneys at Paul, Weiss. Frank was eager to obtain counsel in order to proceed with the English language translation of the diary of Anne Frank. Paul, Weiss has represented Frank family interests in the U. S. to this day (i.e., publication contracts with Doubleday/Random House, the Meyer Levin law suits, rights to Otto Frank's unpublished correspondence)."[64]

Nathan and Helen Straus attended a stage performance of *The Diary of Anne Frank* in 1955 in which Joseph Schildkraut portrayed Otto Frank. After the play Nathan wrote to Schildkraut explaining that he had just witnessed what he considered "one of the highlights of the American theatre in the last half century." "Congratulations on a magnificent portrayal! You have the voice, the manner & the very personality of Otto - who is and was one of my most cherished friends. I am deeply moved ..."[65]

On May 7, 1957 Nathan Jr. wrote, "The news that the people of The Theater Montparnasse in Paris are going to do the "Diary" is thrilling. Of course, I have heard of the tremendous success the play has achieved in Germany and other countries. We had read, also, some brief items that it is to be made into a movie and I hope this will be done in the near future."[66]

Otto responded, "The film contract with Fox [sic] are practically concluded and we shall meet with Mr. George Stevens, who will direct the film end of the week in Amsterdam. You will certainly be interested to hear that there is an "Anne Frank Foundation" has been registered with the purpose to buy the house, in which we were hiding, and to establish an International Youth Center in it. Of course, I am furnishing the funds to buy the house.

"You hardly can imagine the effect the book and the play have in Germany, leading to active help to Jews and to Israel. Already different organizations formed themselves and are doing good work. This is very important as these organizations are fighting also against anti-Semitism which as we all know is still existing and even rising anew."[67]

In 1957 Nathan Straus, Jr. donated $10,000 to the Dutch student housing foundation. He is quoted in a *New York Times* article of July 21st, "The kindness shown by the people of the Netherlands to the victims of the Nazi terror has touched me personally ... Otto Frank, the father of Anne Frank, is one of the oldest friends I have in the world, our friendship dating back to the time when we were both students at Heidelberg University in 1908 and 1909."[68]

He wrote to Otto, "I have arranged, through the Netherland Ambassador in his country, to make a gift on behalf of the Straus Trust to the Central Foundation for Student Housing and have indicated repeatedly that this gift is tied up directly, not only with the larger matter of appreciation for what was done by the people of the Netherland for the victims of Nazi tyranny, but more especially with their kindness to your family – typifying, as it did, the human sympathy that must have been extended to many thousands of others."[69]

In 1957 Otto came to New York with his second wife Fritzi, who was also a Holocaust survivor. They came to attend the trial brought about by the lawsuit filed by Meyer Levin. Nathan served as Otto's character witness.

Nathan Straus Jr.

During that visit Fritzi wrote to their family in Europe, "At noon we went to the countryside, we had been invited by Nathan Straus for the weekend. ... Helen Straus and her eldest son picked us up in their car. We drove to her estate, everything there is like a fairytale or a Hollywood film. ... Helen and Nathan are very amiable. We also got to know their eldest son, his wife and his three children ... Later their second son came along with his wife and child. ... I have to add that all four Straus children were brought up well and did not behave as one would expect from American children."[70]

Family members report that Otto and Fritzi Frank lived with the Strauses on and off for almost two years during the trial. They stayed at the Strauses Westchester County home, Quarry Lake, on the weekends or when the trial was not actively in session and at their New York City apartment whenever it was necessary to be in town. Nathan and Helen's son, R. Peter, became good friends with Otto Frank. He intrviewed him and wrote an article based on that interview.

The lawsuit would take five years to be completely resolved. Levin was awarded $50,000 in damages by the New York State Supreme Court but this verdict was set aside on appeal. Finally the two parties settled, as Levin did not want to proceed with further expensive litigation. The terms of the settlement were never revealed.

Otto Frank spent the rest of his days celebrating the life of his daughter Anne through her words. He wanted them to bring tolerance and compassion to a world that had seen so much hatred and war. And he wanted them to show that the human spirit could not be destroyed.

He had an active correspondence with young people from around the world, many of them becoming fast friends through their letters. He made a point to respond to the many letters he received. Some of this correspondence continued on for years. In each a very personal theme is evident: "do something to help peace, to eliminate prejudice. Begin with your own circle, your own family. Big plans are fine, but prejudice begins with a single individual. Peace is built with very small blocks."[71]

Carl. J. Rheins, former director of New York's YIVO wrote, "Nathan and Helen were true heroes. They fought hard but were defeated by the State Department and a corrupt Cuban regime."[72]

We are saddened by Nathan and Helen Straus' inability to save the Frank family and inspired by their willingness to try, under insurmountable obstacles.

The discovery and declassification of the Otto Frank/Nathan Straus, Jr. letters at YIVO reminds us of the efforts of family members to save their loved ones. And it gives us an opportunity to tell their story.

Otto Frank

Anne wrote in her diary, "I want to go on living even after my death."[73]

Through her letters and through the newly discovered letters between Otto Frank and his friend Nathan Straus Jr., her story, and that of her family, can be retold in a new light. Her wish is granted. Anne and her family will never be forgotten.

After more than fifty years wondering why Otto Frank didn't leave the Netherlands with his family, we finally know the answer. He did try. But it was too late. Otto Frank, an optimist who continued to believe in the goodness of people, did it all *For the Sake of the Children.*

Endnotes

Chapter Two

1. Frank, Otto to Leni Frank Elias. 29 December 1909. (Basel, Switzerland: ANNE FRANK-Fonds)

Chapter Three

2. Mueller, Melissa, with notes by Miep Geis, *Anne Frank: the Biography* (New York, Metropolitan Books, Henry Holt and Company, 1998) page 20
3. Mueller, Melissa, with notes by Miep Geis, *Anne Frank: the Biography* (New York, Metropolitan Books, Henry Holt and Company, 1998) page 32
4. Lee, Carol Ann, *The Hidden Life of Otto Frank* (New York: Perennial, an imprint of HarperCollins, 2002, 2003) page 39
5. Lee, Carol Ann, *The Hidden Life of Otto Frank* (New York: Perennial, an imprint of HarperCollins, 2002, 2003) page 63
6. Mueller, Melissa, with notes by Miep Geis, *Anne Frank: the Biography* (New York, Metropolitan Books, Henry Holt and Company, 1998) page 84
7.Mueller, Melissa, with notes by Miep Geis, Anne Frank: the Biography (New York, Metropolitan Books, Henry Holt and Company, 1998) page 100
8. Frank, Otto to Nathan Straus, Jr. 30 April 1941. (New York: YIVO Institute for Jewish Research, 2007)
9. Lee, Carol Ann, *The Hidden Life of Otto Frank* (New York: Perennial, an imprint of HarperCollins, 2002, 2003) page 81
10. Breitman, Richard, Professor of History, American University, Washington, D.C. 2007. "Blocked By National Security Fears?: The Frank Family and Shifts in American Refugee Policy, 1938-1941. (Prepared for YIVO Institute for Jewish Research, New York: 2007)

11. Engel, David, Greenberg Professor of Holocaust Studies, New York University, New York "Background To The Situation Of Jews In The Netherlands Under Nazi Occupation And of The Family Of Otto Frank." (Prepared for YIVO Institute for Jewish Research, New York: 2007)

12. Engel, David, Greenberg Professor of Holocaust Studies, New York University, New York "Background To The Situation Of Jews In The Netherlands Under Nazi Occupation And of The Family Of Otto Frank." (Prepared for YIVO Institute for Jewish Research, New York: 2007)

Chapter Five

13. Straus, Nathan, Autobiographical Sketch (unpublished, New York City. August 1946) page 3
14. Straus, Nathan, Autobiographical Sketch (unpublished, New York City. August 1946) page 69
15. Straus, Nathan, Autobiographical Sketch (unpublished, New York City, August 1946) page 72
16. Straus, Nathan, Autobiographical Sketch (unpublished, New York City. August 1946) page 122
17. Straus, Nathan, Autobiographical Sketch (unpublished, New York City. August 1946)page 65

Chapter Seven

18. Frank, Otto to Nathan Straus, Jr. 30 April 1941. (New York: YIVO Institute for Jewish Research, 2007)
19. Frank, Otto to Nathan Straus, Jr. 30 April 1941. (New York: YIVO Institute for Jewish Research, 2007)
20. Straus, Helen Sachs, The Shoreham, Washington, D.C. to Augusta Mayerson, Acting Director, Migration Department of the National Refugee Service, 20 May 1941. (New York: YIVO Institute for Jewish Research, 2007)

21. Mayerson, Augusta, Acting Director, Migration Department of the National Refugee Service to Maurice Krinsky, Boston Committee for Refugees, Boston, Massachusetts. 9 June 1941 (New York: YIVO Institute for Jewish Research, 2007)

22. Mayerson, Augusta, Acting Director, Migration Department of the National Refugee Service to Nathan Straus, Jr., 28 June 1941. (New York: YIVO Institute for Jewish Research, 2007)

23. Mayerson, Augusta, Acting Director, Migration Department of the National Refugee Service to Nathan Straus, Jr., The Shoreham, Washington, D.C. 28 June 1941. (New York: YIVO Institute for Jewish Research, 2007)

24. Frank, Otto to Nathan Straus, Jr. 30 June 1941. (New York YIVO Institute for Jewish Research, 2007)

25. Straus, Jr. Nathan to Otto Frank, Amsterdam, Holland. 1 July 1941. (New York: YIVO Institute for Jewish Research, 2007)

26. Mayerson, Augusta, Acting Director, Migration Department of the National Refugee Service to Maurice Krinsky, Boston Committee for Refugees, Boston, Mass. 13 August 1941. (New York: YIVO Institute for Jewish Research, 2007)

27. Straus, Jr. Nathan, to Otto Frank, Amsterdam, Holland. 11 September 1941. (New York: YIVO Institute for Jewish Research, 2007)

28. Frank, Otto, Amsterdam to Nathan Straus, Jr., Washington. 8 September 1941. (New York: YIVO Institute for Jewish Research, 2007)

29. Hollander, Julius, Canton, Mass. to Nathan Straus, Jr., 17 September 1941. (New York: YIVO Institute for Jewish Research, 2007)

30. Mayerson, Augusta, Acting Director, Migration Department of the National Refugee Service to Joodsche Raad Voor, Amsterdam. 19 September 1941. (New York: YIVO Institute for Jewish Research, 2007)

31. Mayerson, Augusta, Acting Director, Migration Department

of the National Refugee Service, New York to Nathan
Straus, Jr., Hotel Shoreham, Washington, D.C. 2 October
1941. (New York: YIVO Institute for Jewish Research,
2007)

32. United States Holocasut Memorial Museum. Holocaust
Encyclopedia. "Voyage of the St. Louis." Internet article.

33. Hollander, Julius, Canton, Mass. to Nathan Straus, Jr., New
York. 6 October 1941. (New York: YIVO Institute for
Jewish Research, 2007)

34. Joodsche Raad Voor Amsterdam, Amsterdam to National
Refugee Service, Inc. New York City. 12 October 1941.
(New York: YIVO Institute for Jewish Research, 2007)

35. Frank, Otto, Amsterdam to Nathan Straus, Jr. 12 October
1941. (New York: YIVO Institute for Jewish Research,
2007)

36. Frank, Otto, Amsterdam to Nathan Straus, Jr. 12 October
1941. (New York: YIVO Institute for Jewish Research,
2007)

37. Mayerson, Augusta, Acting Director, Migration Department
of the National Refugee Service to Julius Hollander,
Canton, Mass. 17 October 1941. (New York: YIVO
Institute for Jewish Research, 2007)

38. Mayerson, Augusta, Acting Director, Migration Department
of the National Refugee Service to Maurice Krinsky,
Executive Secretary, Boston Committee for Refugees,
Boston, Mass. 17 October 1941. (New York: YIVO
Institute for Jewish Research, 2007)

39. Krinsky, Maurice, Executive Secretary, Boston Committee
for Refugees, Boston, Mass. to Augusta Mayerson,
National Refugee Service, New York. 21 October 1941.
(New York: YIVO Institute for Jewish Research, 2007)

40. Krinsky, Maurice, Executive Secretary, Boston Committee
for Refugees, Boston, Mass. to Augusta Mayerson,
National Refugee Service, New York. 21 October 1941.
(New York: YIVO Institute for Jewish Research, 2007)

41. Krinsky, Maurice, Executive Secretary, Boston Committee
for Refugees, Boston, Mass. to Augusta Mayerson,

National Refugee Service, New York. 27 October 1941. (New York: YIVO Institute for Jewish Research, 2007)

42. Mayerson, Augusta, Acting Director, Migration Department of the National Refugee Service, New York to Mrs. Nathan Straus, Jr., Hotel Shoreham, Washington, D.C. 12 November 1941. (New York: YIVO Institute for Jewish Research, 2007)

43. Mayerson, Augusta, Acting Director, Migration Department of the National Refugee Service, New York to Julius Hollander, Canton, Mass. 12 November 1941. (New York: YIVO Institute for Jewish Research, 2007)

44. Hollander, Julius, Canton, Mass. to Mr. and Mrs. Nathan Straus, New York City. 18 November 1941. (New York: YIVO Institute for Jewish Research, 2007)

45. Hollander, Julius, Canton, Mass. to National Refugee Service, New York City, New York. 22 November 1941. (New York: YIVO Institute for Jewish Research, 2007)

46. ST. (Interoffice Memo) RE: Otto Frank 27 November 1941. (New York: YIVO Institute for Jewish Research, 2007)

47. Mayerson, Augusta, to Julius Hollander, Canton, Mass. 27 November 1941. (New York: YIVO Institute for Jewish Research, 2007)

48. Hollander, Julius, Canton, Mass. to Miss Augusta Mayerson, National Refugee Service, New York. 27 November 1941. (New York: YIVO Institute for Jewish Research, 2007)

49. Hollander, Julius, Canton, Mass. to Miss Augusta Mayerson, National Refugee Service, New York. 27 November 1941. (New York: YIVO Institute for Jewish Research, 2007)

50. ST (Interoffice Memo) to Augusta Mayerson, National Refugee Service, New York. 11 December 1941. (New York: YIVO Institute for Jewish Research, 2007)

51. Breitman, Richard, Professor of History, American University, Washington, D.C. 2007. "Blocked By National Security Fears?: The Frank Family and Shifts in American Refugee Policy, 1938-1941. (Prepared for

YIVO Institute for Jewish Research, New York: 2007)
52 Wyman, David S., *Paper Walls: America and the Refugee Crisis 1938-1941* (Amherst MA, University of Massachusetts Press, 1968) page X

Chapter Eight

53. Petluck, Ann S., Director, Migration Department, National Refugee Service, New York to Mr. Arthur D. Greenleigh, New York. 26 June 1945. (New York: YIVO Institute for Jewish Research, 2007)
54. Frank, Otto to Nathan Straus, Jr. New York. 24 September 1945. (Amsterdam, Netherlands: Anne Frank House)
55. Frank, Otto to Nathan Straus, Jr., WMCA, 1657 Broadway, New York 19, N.Y. 24 September 1945. (Amsterdam, Netherlands: Anne Frank House)
56. Straus, Jr., Nathan, New York to Otto Frank. 25 October 1945. (Amsterdam, Netherlands: Anne Frank House)
57. Frank, Otto to Nathan Straus, Jr. WMCA, 1657 Broadway, New York 19, N.Y. 14 November 1945. (Amsterdam, Netherlands: Anne Frank House)
58. Petluck, Ann S., Director, Migration Department, National Refugee Service, New York to Julius Hollander, New York. 31 January 1946. (New York: YIVO Institute for Jewish Research, 2007)
59. Hollander, Julius to unknown recipient. 2 February 1946. (New York: YIVO Institute for Jewish Research, 2007)
60. Straus, Jr., Nathan, WMCA, 1657 Broadway, New York 19, N.Y. to Otto Frank. 15 May 1952. (Amsterdam, Netherlands: Anne Frank House)
61. Straus, Helen Sachs, "Quarry Lake," Quarry Heights, White Plains, N.Y. to Otto Frank. 9 July 1946. (Amsterdam, Netherlands: Anne Frank House)
62. Frank, Otto to Helen Sachs Straus, New York. 13 July 1952. (Amsterdam, Netherlands: Anne Frank House)
63. Straus, Jr., Nathan, WMCA, 1657 Broadway, New York 19, N.Y. to Otto Frank. 15 January 1953. (Amsterdam,

Netherlands: Anne Frank House)

64. Rheins, Carl J., former Director of YIVO Institute for Jewish Research, New York to Joan Adler, Executive Director, Straus Historical Society, Inc. Smithtown. NY. 2007.

65. Straus, Jr., Nathan, New York to Joseph Schildkraut. 1955. (New York: Straus Historical Society, Inc.)

66. Straus, Jr., Nathan, WMCA, 1657 Broadway, New York 19, N.Y. to Otto Frank. 7 May 1957. (Amsterdam, Netherlands: Anne Frank House)

67. Frank, Otto, Herbstgasse 11, Basle to Nathan Straus, Jr., New York. 22 May 1957. (Amsterdam, Netherlands: Anne Frank House)

68. Waggoner, Walter H., "New Yorker Aids Dutch Students," *The New York Times*, 21 July 1957. Page 19.

69. Straus, Jr., Nathan, WMCA, 1657 Broadway, New York 19, N.Y. to Otto Frank. 26 June 1957. (Amsterdam, Netherlands: Anne Frank House)

70. Frank, Fritzi, to All My Loved Ones. 18 November 1957. (Basel, Switzerland: ANNE FRANK-Fonds)

71. Straus, R. Peter, "His Message Is His Mission: The Father of Anne's Frank's Diary." New York. 1975

72. Rheins, Carl J., former Director of YIVO Institute for Jewish Research, New York to Joan Adler, Executive Director, Straus Historical Society, Inc. Smithtown. NY. 1 February 2007

73. Frank, Anne. *The Diary of a Young Girl*. (New York: Anchor Books) 1991

Bibliography

Books

Beir, Robert L. with Brian Josepher, *Roosevelt and the Holocaust: A Rooseveltian Examines the Policies and Remembers the Times* (Fort Lee, New Jersey: Barricade, 2006)

Crowe, David M., *The Holocaust: Roots, History and Aftermath* (Philadelphia, PA, Westview Press, 2008)

Frank, Otto, and Mirjam Pressler, editors, *The Diary of a Young Girl* (The Definitive Edition) (New York, Anchor books, a division of Random House, Inc., 1991)

Lee, Carol Ann, *The Hidden Life of Otto Frank* (New York: Perennial, an imprint of HarperCollins, 2002, 2003)

Lindwer, Willy, Translated from the Dutch by Alison Meersschaert, *The Last Seventh Months of Anne Frank* (New York, Anchor Books, Double day, 1988)

Moore, Bob, *Victims & Survivors: The Nazi Persecution of the Jews in the Netherlands 1940 - 1945* (New York: Arnold, Hodder Headline Group, St. Martin's Press, 1997)

Mueller, Melissa, with notes by Miep Geis, *Anne Frank: the biography* (New York, Metropolitan Books, Henry Holt and Company, 1998)

Rubin, Susan Goldman, *Searching For Anne Frank: Letters from Amsterdam to Iowa* (New York, Harry N. Abrams Publishers, 2003)

Rubin, Susan Goldman, illustrated by Bill Fransworth, *The Anne Frank Case: Simon Wiesenthal's Search for the Truth* (New York, Holiday House, 2009)

Tonge, Neil, *Documenting World War II: The Holocaust* (New York, Rosen Central, 2009)

Van der Rol, Ruud and Rian Verhoeven for the Anne Frank House, *Anne Frank: Beyond the Diary, A Photographic Remembrance* (New York, Puffin Books, 1995)

Wyman, David S., Paper Walls: *America and the Refugee Crisis 1938-1941* (Amherst MA, University of Massachusetts Press, 1968)

Wyman, David S., *The Abandonment of the Jews: America and the Holocaust 1941-1945* (New York, Pantheon Books, 1984)

Articles

Backman, Marjorie, "Otto Frank's Hunt for a Visa," *Time Magazine.* 16 February 2007.

Bone, James, "Anne Frank Family Sought Refuge in US," *The Australian.* 15 February 2007.

Breitman, Richard, Professor of History, American University. "Blocked by National Security Fears?: The Frank Family and Shifts in American Refugee Policy, 1938-1941." Prepared for YIVO Institute for Jewish Research, RE: Otto Frank. 14 February 2007.

Cohen, Patricia, "In Old Files, Fading Hopes of Anne Frank's Family. *New York Times.* 15 February 2007. Page A1.

Engel, David, "Background to the Situation of Jews in the Netherlands Under Nazi Occupation and of the Family of Otto Frank." Prepared for YIVO Institute for Jewish Research, RE: Otto Frank. 14 February 2007.

Feldman, Ellen, "Anne Frank in America," American Heritage. February/March 2005. Pages 56 - 62. (Found at the FDR Presidential Library, Hyde Park, NY)

Press Release: "Newly Discovered File Documents Efforts of Anne Frank's Father to Escape from Nazi-Occupied Holland," YIVO Institute for Jewish Research, 15 West 16th Street, New York, NY 10011. 14 February 2007.

Time, CNN, "Zion, Ten Years After," (online article) Monday, April 4, 1932.

Internet Article

(http://www.jphs.org/locales/2005/10/15/bromley-heath-public-housing-development-history.html)

Unpublished Papers

Straus, Nathan, Autobiographical Sketch (unpublished, New York City, August 1946)

Transcript

WCBS Editorial # 88: Nathan Straus – In Memoriam, Date and Time of Broadcast 14 September 1961, 12:15 P.M. and 11: 15 P.M.

Letters, Postcards, Telegrams, Interoffice Memoranda and Forms

Frank, Otto to Dear Charley. 30 April 1941. YIVO: Institute for Jewish Research, 15 West 16 Street, New York, NY 10011

Straus, Helen Sachs, The Shoreham, Connecticut Avenue at Calvert Street, Washington, D.C. to Miss Mayerson. 28 May. YIVO: Institute for Jewish Research, 15 West 16 Street, New York, NY 10011

Mayerson, Augusta, Acting Director, Migration Department to Mr. Nathan Straus, The Shoreham, Connecticut Avenue at Calvert Street, Washington, D.C. 3 June 1941. YIVO: Institute for Jewish Research, 15 West 16 Street, New York, NY 10011

Mayerson, National Refugee Service, Inc., Interoffice Memorandum to Miss Susan Kramer. 3 June 1941. YIVO: Institute for Jewish Research, 15 West 16 Street, New York, NY 10011

Mayerson Augusta, Acting Director, Migration Department to Mr. Maurice Krinsky, Boston Committee for Refugees, 24 Province Street, Boston, Massachusetts. 9 June 1941. YIVO: Institute for Jewish Research, 15 West 16 Street, New York, NY 10011

Rogan, E. M., Secretary to Mr. Nathan Straus, 630 Sixth Avenue, New York City to Miss Augusta Mayerson, Migration Department, National Refugee Service, 165 West 46th

Street, New York City. 11 June 1941. YIVO: Institute for Jewish Research, 15 West 16 Street, New York, NY 10011

Krinsky, Maurice, Boston Committee for Refugees, 24 Province Street, Boston, Mass. to Miss Susan Kramer, National Refugee Service, 165 West 46th Street, New York City. 16 June 1941. YIVO: Institute for Jewish Research, 15 West 16 Street, New York, NY 10011

Mayerson, Augusta, Acting Director, Migration Department to Miss E. M. Rogan, Secretary to Mr. Nathan Straus, 630 Sixth Avenue, New York City. 18 June 1941. YIVO: Institute for Jewish Research, 15 West 16 Street, New York, NY 10011

Mayerson, Augusta, Acting Director, Migration Department to Mr. Nathan Straus, The Shoreham, Connecticut Avenue at Calvert Street, Washington, D.C. 25 June 1941. YIVO: Institute for Jewish Research, 15 West 16 Street, New York, NY 10011

Straus, Nathan to Otto Frank, Nerwedeplein 37, Amsterdam, Holland. 1 July 1941. YIVO: Institute for Jewish Research, 15 West 16 Street, New York, NY 10011

Kramer, S. Summary Case #A23,007. 12 August 1941. YIVO: Institute for Jewish Research, 15 West 16 Street, New York, NY 10011

Mayerson, Augusta, Acting Director, Migration Department to Mr. Maurice Krinsky, Boston Committee for Refugees, 24 Province Street, Boston, Mass. 17 August 1941. YIVO: Institute for Jewish Research, 15 West 16 Street, New York, NY 10011

Frank, Otto, Merwedeplein 37, Amsterdam to Dear Charley. 8 September 1941. YIVO: Institute for Jewish Research, 15 West 16 Street, New York, NY 10011

Straus, Nathan to Otto Frank, Nerwedeplein 37, Amsterdam, Holland. 11 September 1941. YIVO: Institute for Jewish Research, 15 West 16 Street, New York, NY 10011

Mayerson, Acting Director, Migration Department to Miss E. M. Rogan, Secretary to Mr. Nathan Straus, 630 Sixth Avenue, New York City. 11 September 1941. YIVO:

Institute for Jewish Research, 15 West 16 Street, New
York, NY 10011

Hollander, Julius, 138 High Street, Canton, Mass. to Mr. Strauss.
17 September 1941. YIVO: Institute for Jewish Research,
15 West 16 Street, New York, NY 10011

Garten, S., Summary: Case #A23,007. 10 September 1941. YIVO:
Institute for Jewish Research, 15 West 16 Street, New
York, NY 10011

Rogan, E. M., Secretary to Mr. Nathan Straus, 630 Sixth Avenue,
New York City to Miss Augusta Mayerson, National
Refugee Service, Inc., 165 West 46th Street, New York
City. 17 November 1941. YIVO: Institute for Jewish
Research, 15 West 16 Street, New York, NY 10011

Krinsky, Maurice, Executive Secretary, Boston Committee for
Refugees, 24 Province Street, Boston, Mass. to Miss
Susan Kramer, National Refugee Service, 165 West 46th
Street, New York City. 20 September 1941. YIVO:
Institute for Jewish Research, 15 West 16 Street, New
York, NY 10011

Mayerson, National Refugee Service Inc., 165 West 46th Street,
New York to Joodsche Raad Voor, Amsterdam.
Telegram. 22 September 1941. YIVO: Institute for
Jewish Research, 15 West 16 Street, New York, NY 10011

Mayerson Augusta, Migration Dept. to Comvluch, Amsterdam.
Postal Telegraph. 19 September 1941. YIVO: Institute for
Jewish Research, 15 West 16 Street, New York, NY 10011

Kramer, Susan, National Refugee Service, Inc., Interoffice
Memorandum to Miss Augusta Mayerson, Migration
Dept. 29 September 1941. YIVO: Institute for Jewish
Research, 15 West 16 Street, New York, NY 10011

Mayerson, Augusta, Acting Director, Migration Department,
National Refugee Service, Inc. 165 West 46th Street, New
York City to Mr. Nathan Straus, Hotel Shoreham,
Connecticut Avenue at Calvert Street, Washington, D.C.
2 October 1941. YIVO: Institute for Jewish Research, 15
West 16 Street, New York, NY 10011

Mayerson, Augusta, Acting Director, Migration Department to

Mr. Maurice Krinsky, Executive Secretary, Boston
Committee for Refugees, 24 Province Street, Boston,
Massachusetts. 3 October 1941. YIVO: Institute for
Jewish Research, 15 West 16 Street, New York, NY 10011

Hollander, Julius, 138 High Street, Canton, Mass. to Mr. Nathan
Straus, 630 Sixth Avenue, New York, N.Y. 6 October
1941. YIVO: Institute for Jewish Research, 15 West 16
Street, New York, NY 10011

Straus, Helen S. to unknown recipient. 10 October 1941. YIVO:
Institute for Jewish Research, 15 West 16 Street, New
York, NY 10011

National Refugee Service, Inc., 165 West 46th Street, New York
City to Joodsche Raad Voor, Amsterdam. 12 October
1941. YIVO: Institute for Jewish Research, 15 West 16
Street, New York, NY 10011

Joodsche Raad Voor Amsterdam 12 October 1941. YIVO:
Institute for Jewish Research, 15 West 16 Street, New
York, NY 10011

Frank, Otto to Dear Charley, 12 October 1941. YIVO: Institute
for Jewish Research, 15 West 16 Street, New York, NY
10011

Mayerson, Augusta, Acting Director, Migration Department to
Mr. Julius Hollander, 138 High Street, Canton, Mass. 17
October 1941. YIVO: Institute for Jewish Research, 15
West 16 Street, New York, NY 10011

Mayerson, Augusta, Acting Director, Migration Department to
Mr. Maurice Krinsky, Executive Secretary, Boston
Committee for Refugees, 24 Province Street, Boston,
Mass. 17 October 1941. YIVO: Institute for Jewish
Research, 15 West 16 Street, New York, NY 10011

Mayerson, Augusta, Acting Director, Migration Department to
Mr. Nathan Straus, Hotel Shoreham, Washington, D.C.
17 October 1941. YIVO: Institute for Jewish Research, 15
West 16 Street, New York, NY 10011

Krinsky, Maurice, Executive Secretary, Boston Committee for
Refugees, 24 Province Street, Boston, Mass. to Miss
Augusta Mayerson, National Refugee Service, 165 West

46th Street, New York, New York. 21 October 1941.
YIVO: Institute for Jewish Research, 15 West 16 Street,
New York, NY 10011

Kramer, Susan to Augusta Mayerson. Memo. undated. YIVO:
Institute for Jewish Research, 15 West 16 Street, New
York, NY 10011

Krinsky, Maurice, Executive Secretary, Boston Committee for
Refugees, 24 Province Street, Boston, Mass. to Miss
Augusta Mayerson, National Refugee Service, 165 West
46th Street, New York, New York. 27 October 1941.
YIVO: Institute for Jewish Research, 15 West 16 Street,
New York, NY 10011

Razovsky, Cecilia, National Refugee Service, Inc., Interoffice
Memorandum. 30 October 1941. YIVO: Institute for
Jewish Research, 15 West 16 Street, New York, NY 10011

Mayerson, Augusta, Acting Director, Migration Department to
Mr. Maurice Krinsky, Executive Secretary, Boston
Committee for Refugees, 24 Province Street, Boston,
Mass. 1 November 1941. YIVO: Institute for Jewish
Research, 15 West 16 Street, New York, NY 10011

Mayerson, Augusta, Acting Director, Migration Department to
Mr. Nathan Straus, Hotel Shoreham, Washington, D.C.
1 November 1941. YIVO: Institute for Jewish Research,
15 West 16 Street, New York, NY 10011

Mayerson, Augusta, Acting Director, Migration Department to
Mr. Nathan Straus, Hotel Shoreham, Washington, D.C.
12 November 1941. YIVO: Institute for Jewish Research,
15 West 16 Street, New York, NY 10011

Mayerson, Augusta, Acting Director, Migration Department to
Mr. Maurice Krinsky, Executive Secretary, Boston
Committee for Refugees, 24 Province Street, Boston,
Mass. 12 November 1941. YIVO: Institute for Jewish
Research, 15 West 16 Street, New York, NY 10011

Mayerson, Augusta, Acting Director, Migration Department to
Julius Hollander, 138 High Street, Canotn, Mass. 12
November 1941. YIVO: Institute for Jewish Research, 15
West 16 Street, New York, NY 10011

Straus, Helen S., Federal Works Agency, United States Housing Authority, Washington to Miss Mayerson. 12 November 1941. YIVO: Institute for Jewish Research, 15 West 16 Street, New York, NY 10011

Krinsky, Maurice, Executive Secretary, Boston Committee for Refugees, 24 Province Street, Boston, Mass. to Miss Augusta Mayerson, Acting Director, Migration Dept., National Refugee Service, 165 West 46th Street, New York, N.Y. 17 November 1941. YIVO: Institute for Jewish Research, 15 West 16 Street, New York, NY 10011

Hollander, Julius, 138 High Street, Canton, Mass. to Mr. & Mrs. Nathan Straus, Suite 708, 165 West 46th Street, New York City. 18 November 1941. YIVO: Institute for Jewish Research, 15 West 16 Street, New York, NY 10011

Mayerson, National Refugee Service to Mr. Maurice Krinsky, Boston Committee for Refugees, 24 Province Street, Boston, Mass. Telegram. 21 November 1941. YIVO: Institute for Jewish Research, 15 West 16 Street, New York, NY 10011

Mae: Memorandum. 21 November 1941. YIVO: Institute for Jewish Research, 15 West 16 Street, New York, NY 10011. YIVO: Institute for Jewish Research, 15 West 16 Street, New York, NY 10011

Hollander, Julius, 138 High Street, Canton, Mass. to National Refugee Service, 165 West 46th Street, New York City, New York. 22 November 1941. YIVO: Institute for Jewish Research, 15 West 16 Street, New York, NY 10011

ST: Memorandum. 27 November 1941. YIVO: Institute for Jewish Research, 15 West 16 Street, New York, NY 10011

Mayerson, Augusta to Mr. Julius Hollander, 138 High Street, Canton, Mass. Telegram. 27 November 1941. YIVO: Institute for Jewish Research, 15 West 16 Street, New York, NY 10011

Hollander, Julius, 138 High Street, Canton, Mass. to Miss Augusta Mayerson, National Refugee Service, 165 West 46th Street, New York City, New York. 27 November 1941. YIVO: Institute for Jewish Research, 15 West 16

Street, New York, NY 10011

Hollander, Julius, 138 High Street, Canton, Mass. to Miss Augusta Mayerson, National Refugee Service, 165 West 46th Street, New York City, New York. 28 November 1941. YIVO: Institute for Jewish Research, 15 West 16 Street, New York, NY 10011

Krinsky, Maurice, Executive Secretary, Boston Committee for Refugees, 24 Province Street, Boston, Mass. to Miss Augusta Mayerson, National Refugee Service, 165 West 46th Street, New York City. 1 December 1941. YIVO: Institute for Jewish Research, 15 West 16 Street, New York, NY 10011

Reesh: Memo to unnamed recipient. 2 December 1941. YIVO: Institute for Jewish Research, 15 West 16 Street, New York, NY 10011

ST: National Refugee Servicce, Inc., Interoffice Memorandum Telephone Message to Miss Augusta Mayerson. 11 December 1941. YIVO: Institute for Jewish Research, 15 West 16 Street, New York, NY 10011

Saxl, G. V., Memo. Case #A 23,007. 22 August 1945. YIVO: Institute for Jewish Research, 15 West 16 Street, New York, NY 10011

Inquiry: Mr. Hollander, 31 W 71 St. 14 June 1945. YIVO: Institute for Jewish Research, 15 West 16 Street, New York, NY 10011

Migration Department Fact Sheet: Clients Still Abroad. Case Name: Frank. Case Worker: G. V. Saxl. Case Opened 29 May 1941. YIVO: Institute for Jewish Research, 15 West 16 Street, New York, NY 10011

Petluck, Ann S., Director, Migration Department to Mr. Julius Hollander, 31 West 71 Street, New York 23, N.Y. 15 June 1945. YIVO: Institute for Jewish Research, 15 West 16 Street, New York, NY 10011

Petluck, Ann S., Director, Migration Department to Mr. Arthur D. Greenleigh, APO # 887, % Postmaster, New York. 26 June 1945. YIVO: Institute for Jewish Research, 15 West 16 Street, New York, NY 10011

Hollander, Julius, 31 W 71 St., New York 23, N.Y. to Gentlemen, National Refugee Service, Inc., New York City. 29 June. YIVO: Institute for Jewish Research, 15 West 16 Street, New York, NY 10011

Frank, Otto, to Dear Charly. 24 September 1945. Anne Frank Stichting, Postbus 730, 10000 AS Amsterdam.

Frank, Otto. Undated. Anne Frank Stichting, Postbus 730, 10000 AS Amsterdam.

Central Location Index, Inc., 165 West 46th Street, New York 19 to Miss B. Rapaport, NRS, and to Mrs. E. Kanitz, NCJW. Notification of Location (Possible). 24 October 1945. YIVO: Institute for Jewish Research, 15 West 16 Street, New York, NY 10011

Straus, Nathan, wmca, 1657 Broadway, New York 19, N.Y. to Mr. Otto Frank, N.V. Nederlandsche-Opekat Mij., Prinsengracht 263, Amsterdam C, Holland. 25 October 1945. Anne Frank Stichting, Postbus 730, 10000 AS Amsterdam.

Frank, Otto to Mr. Nathan Straus, WMCA Inc., 1657 Broadway, New York. 14 November 1945. Anne Frank Stichting, Postbus 730, 10000 AS Amsterdam.

Eglin, Harry, Personal Inquiry Dept., American Joint Distribution Committee, 19, Rue De Teheran, Paris (8) to National Refugee Service, 105 Nassau Street, New York 7, N.Y. 30 November 1945. YIVO: Institute for Jewish Research, 15 West 16 Street, New York, NY 10011

Petluck, Ann S., Director, Migration Department to Mr. Julius Hollander, 31 West 71 Street, New York 23, N.Y. 31 January 1946. YIVO: Institute for Jewish Research, 15 West 16 Street, New York, NY 10011

Hollander, Julius to Gentlemen. 2 February 1946. YIVO: Institute for Jewish Research, 15 West 16 Street, New York, NY 10011

Petluck, Ann S., Director, Migration Department to Mr. Julius Hollander, 31 West 71 Street, New York 23, N.Y. 6 February 1946. YIVO: Institute for Jewish Research, 15 West 16 Street, New York, NY 10011

Central Location Index, Inc., to Mrs. E. Kanitz, NCJW. and to
Miss B. Rapaport, NRS. Notification of Location
(Possible). Location Unit. 1 May 1946. YIVO: Institute
for Jewish Research, 15 West 16 Street, New York, NY
10011

National Refugee Service, Inc., 139 Centre Street, New York
13, N.Y. Application for Location Service. 26 July 1946.
YIVO: Institute for Jewish Research, 15 West 16 Street,
New York, NY 10011

Straus, Nathan, wmca, 1657 Broadway, New York 19, N.Y. to Mr.
Otto Frank, Prinsengracht 263, Amsterdam, Holland. 15
May 1952. Anne Frank Stichting, Postbus 730, 10000 AS
Amsterdam.

Straus, Helen Sachs, "Quarry Lake," Quarry Heights, White
Plains, N.Y. to Otto. 9 July 1952. Anne Frank Stichting,
Postbus 730, 10000 AS Amsterdam.

Frank, Otto to Dear Helen, 13 May 1952. Anne Frank Stichting,
Postbus 730, 10000 AS Amsterdam.

Straus, Helen Sachs, "Quarry Lake," Quarry Heights, White
Plains, N.Y. to Otto. 18 July. Anne Frank Stichting,
Postbus 730, 10000 AS Amsterdam.

Frank, Otto to Dear Helen, 28 July 1952. Anne Frank Stichting,
Postbus 730, 10000 AS Amsterdam

Straus, Nathan, wmca, 1657 Broadway, New York 19, N.Y. to Mr.
Otto Frank, St. Moritz Bad, Switzerland. 15 January 1953.
Anne Frank Stichting, Postbus 730, 10000 AS
Amsterdam

Helen to Otto, undated. Anne Frank Stichting, Postbus 730,
10000 AS Amsterdam

Straus, Nathan, wmca, 1657 Broadway, New York 19, N.Y. to Mr.
Otto Frank,"Trottehoefli," Beckenried b/Luzern,
Switzerland. 27 May 1953. Anne Frank Stichting, Postbus
730, 10000 AS Amsterdam.

Frank, Otto, Beckenried to Nathan. 7 September 1953. Anne
Frank Stichting, Postbus 730, 10000 AS Amsterdam.

Straus, Nathan, wmca, 1657 Broadway, New York 19, N.Y. to Mr.
Otto Frank,"Trottehoefli," Beckenried b/Luzern,

Switzerland. 16 May 1953. Anne Frank Stichting, Postbus 730, 10000 AS Amsterdam.

Booker, L. wmca, 1657 Broadway, New York 19, N.Y. to Mr. Otto Frank, Herbstgasse 11, Basel, Switzerland. 9 February 1954. Anne Frank Stichting, Postbus 730, 10000 AS Amsterdam.

Straus, Nathan, wmca, 1657 Broadway, New York 19, N.Y. to Mr. Otto Frank, Herbstgasse 11, Basel, Switzerland. 7 May 1957. Anne Frank Stichting, Postbus 730, 10000 AS Amsterdam.

Frank, Otto, Herbstgasse 11, Basel to Nathan. 22 May 1957. Anne Frank Stichting, Postbus 730, 10000 AS Amsterdam.

Straus, Nathan, wmca, 1657 Broadway, New York 19, N.Y. to Mr. Otto Frank, Herbstgasse 11, Basel, Switzerland. 28 May 1957. Anne Frank Stichting, Postbus 730, 10000 AS Amsterdam.

Straus, Nathan, wmca, 1657 Broadway, New York 19, N.Y. to Mr. Otto Frank, Herbstgasse 11, Basel, Switzerland. 16 June 1957. Anne Frank Stichting, Postbus 730, 10000 AS Amsterdam.

Straus, Nathan, wmca, 1657 Broadway, New York 19, N.Y. to Mr. Otto Frank, Hotel Meurice, 145 West 58th Street, New York 19, New York. 24 December 1957. Anne Frank Stichting, Postbus 730, 10000 AS Amsterdam.

Straus, Nathan, wmca, 1657 Broadway, New York 19, N.Y. to Mr. Otto Frank, Herbstgasse 11, Basel, Switzerland. 8 July 1958. Anne Frank Stichting, Postbus 730, 10000 AS Amsterdam.

Straus, Nathan, wmca, 1657 Broadway, New York 19, N.Y. to Mr Otto Frank, Herbstgasse 11, Basel, Switzerland. 8 October 1958. Anne Frank Stichting, Postbus 730, 10000 AS Amsterdam.

Audio Book

Gies, Miep and Alison Leslie Gold. Anne Frank Remembered.

Read by Barbara Rosenblat. Springwater, an imprint of Oasis Audio.

CPSIA information can be obtained at www.ICGtesting.com
Printed in the USA
LVOW06*0047150814

399239LV00002B/2/P

9 780980 125054